THE FLOWERING OF BRITAIN

THE FLOWERING OF BRITAIN

Richard Mabey and Tony Evans

New Edition

Chatto & Windus
London

Published in 1989 by
Chatto & Windus Ltd
30 Bedford Square
London WC1B 3SG

First published 1980
Hutchinson & Co (Publishers) Ltd

A CIP catalogue record of this book is available from the
British Library.

ISBN 0 7011 3456 9

Designed by Shireen Nathoo

Photoset by Rowland Phototypesetting Ltd
Bury St Edmunds, Suffolk
Printed in Great Britain

FRONTISPIECE
*The flowering of Britain – the first
sea campions of spring.
Pembrokeshire*

Contents

Acknowledgements

Our warm thanks for advice, help and hospitality to:

T. Beardsley; Berkhamsted and District Local History Society; the Berkshire, Buckinghamshire and Oxfordshire Naturalists' Trust; Percy Birtchnell; Ronald Blythe; the Botanical Society of the British Isles; Jean Buchanan; Susan Campbell; Judith Church of C.A.B.S.; Clun Town Trust; Gigi Crompton; Evangeline Dickson; John Dony; David Dymond; Francesca Greenoak; Robin and Rachel Hamilton; Brian Jackman; the Kenneth Allsop Memorial Trust; Noel King; the President of Magdalen College, Oxford; Edgar Milne-Redhead; the Nature Conservancy Council; Bronwen Nixon; the Norfolk Naturalists' Trust; Philip Oswald; Frank Perring; George Peterken; Jane Puzey of R.S.N.C.; Oliver Rackham; Jamie Robertson; Francis Rose; Peter Schofield; Charles Sinker; The Suffolk Trust for Nature Conservation; Derek Wells; Stan Woodell.

List of Plates

Preface

The Flowering of Britain was first published almost ten years ago – as long a time in the life of the environment, these days, as it is in the life of a human. Enough has happened to make a policy of thoroughgoing revision more than usually tempting for this new edition – a clean sweep not just of errors and slipshod writing, but obsolete opinions and rushed judgements. But reading it through again I was struck by how little I could bear to change, and how much I missed the mood the book had tried to catch. Perhaps the passing of ten years always brings on this kind of nostalgia.

Yet I think that there have been changes in our confidence about the natural world as well as in our attitudes towards it. To the extent that one can stand back from one's own writing, *Flowering* now reads to me like a book written in the sunshine. In one sense this was literally true. The mid-seventies, when Tony and I did most of our field-work, were remarkable for their mild winters and for the two exceptional Mediterranean summers of 1975 and 76. Yet there is also an optimism about it that I think would be hard to capture now. Although the seventies was the period in which we began to wake up to the appalling damage which intensive agriculture had done to our countryside and its wild flowers, it was also one of excitement and enthusiasm. Many of us 'discovered' ecology at this time, and with it the idea that even in Britain nature and culture had complex and ancient intertwinings. This understanding brought with it a kind of faith in the resilience of the living world: down in the parish it would always be possible to see off the land-grabbers and wood-wreckers.

These days the world seems a smaller and grimmer place. Acid rain and the warming of the earth from the greenhouse effect will not be put right so easily and are already having insidious effects on our ecology. The prospect of olive groves on the Sussex Downs is no real consolation for the catastrophes that already seem inevitable elsewhere.

But there may just be a hopeful lesson in the fortunes of our own flora, though the losses, it hardly needs pointing out, still proceed inexorably, especially at a local level. Orchid fields continue to vanish under speculative building. Fen flowers still retreat before the tide of sewage and nitrates that pours down our watercourses. Yet many of the worst excesses of the nineteen-seventies have been brought under control. Ancient woodlands now have many friends and a measure, at least, of financial and legal protection. Wayside verges are cut less obsessively and sprayed almost never. The elms are reappearing. Even agriculture seems to have adopted a more environmentally enlightened attitude in the face of the surpluses scandal.

There has also been a continuing spread of the escapes and immigrants that have always replenished our native flora; some none too welcome, like the now firmly entrenched Japanese knotweed; some as dazzlingly odd as the continental gentian that blow on just one Chiltern hillside. And a few that look like becoming permanent bright additions, like the bearded irises now spreading along west London railway embankments.

It is the way that plants like these – native or naturalized – enhance our sense of place that I find increasingly heartening. If Tony and I were producing the book now there would be more on this, especially on the landscapes and plants of limestone, a magnanimous, adaptable and life-giving rock that we explored briefly in Ireland in 1977 (p.158). We would want to include the Yorkshire Dales, too, with their limestone pavements studded with lilies-of-the-valley and bird's-eye primroses, and the cryptic fastnesses of the Mendips, where meadow saffron and the startling deep-blue flowers of purple gromwell glow in the woods. All such places gain part of their distinctiveness from plants, from their familiar flashes of colour in their seasons, and their dogged persistence over history. They are part of what makes one place different from another.

The Flowering of Britain tried to catch, albeit in a very personal way, something

---

of the growing awareness of these cultural relations between plant and place and season, when we were aware of the threats but not yet too pessimistic about them. Which is why, apart from correcting mistakes and inelegant phrasings, and adding a few footnotes, I have left the text as it was written. I would like to think that the story it tells might still have the power to lift the spirits in these gloomy times as it did Tony's and mine when we were unravelling it.

Richard Mabey, December 1988

PART ONE

Introduction

THE ORCHID AND THE PHOTOGRAPHERS

I think the summer of 1975 must take a good deal of the credit for reawakening our affections for our native wild flowers. Memories for weather are notoriously short, but I doubt if many people have forgotten the heat-wave that began early that June and stretched in an almost unbroken succession of blazing, burnished days into the middle of September. The forecasters, who had consigned hot summers to the past, were confounded; tropical yuccas bloomed in the home counties, and many farmers were so short of grass that they took to haymaking on the roadside verges. Yet, throughout much of the country, local government economies meant that our wayside flowers were spared their usual obsessive shearings, and they bloomed with a profusion and variety that had not been seen for a generation. At the end of the summer they were additionally blessed by the passing of a wild plants protection bill. It may have been no coincidence that one of the flowers specially mentioned in this bill, the military orchid, had symbolically opened the whole brilliant pageant by appearing in close-up in the *Daily Mirror*, on a page usually reserved for pin-ups.

The story behind the military orchid's moment of glory has all the qualities of a good romantic fable. Once, when all the summers were golden no doubt, it had flourished on the chalk hills of southern England, in homely, familiar countryside. There had been a colony at the bottom of the slope beneath the Earl of Bridgewater's monument at Ashridge. In Essex it had grown 'on a little hillock in the corner of a ploughed field adjoining the way leading from Goldington Hall by the lime kiln towards Gestingthorpe'. *Orchis militaris* is hardly a formal beauty – at least not in a florist's sense – but its blooms are distinctive enough to have been known and named as far back as the sixteenth century. John Gerard was the first to describe it in print in 1597. He mentions two 'soldier' orchids – 'Souldiers Cullions' (literally 'soldiers' testicles' – from the shape of the bulb) which, from the accompanying illustration, I take to be our military orchid, and 'Souldiers Satyrion', which seems to correspond to our lady orchid, *Orchis purpurea*. The individual blooms of both species are similarly remarkable, and in his account Gerard describes how they acquired their common soldierly epithet:

> Souldiers Satyrion bringeth forth many large and ribbed leaves . . . among which riseth up a fat stalke full of sap or juyce, clothed or wrapped in the like leaves even to the tuft of floures, whereupon do grow little floures resembling a little man having a helmet upon his head, his hands and legges cut off.
>
> *The Herball*

But the military orchid is a plant of the warm south, on the very edge of its range here, and even where it was plentiful it would only appear erratically. Some seasons it would flower, some not. It took four years for the minute seed to push a stalk above ground, another four for a flower to appear. Perhaps it was this temperamentalness, aggravated by human disturbance or a worsening climate, that sparked off the decline of the military orchid in the latter half of the nineteenth century. No one is really sure. But it began to disappear from one district after another, and by the turn of the century was all but extinct in Britain. The last reliable records are from 1914. For the next thirty years it was not seen – or at least not reported – by a single human soul. Had it truly become extinct, or were its sensitive seeds going through a period of dormancy? The even more romantic possibility that it was still blooming in some unexplored corner of the Chilterns turned searching for the Lost Soldiers into something of an obsession for orchid lovers. Most of the old sites and many potentially new ones were visited in the hope that one hot summer it would reappear.

In the end it was found almost by chance by an amateur botanist out for a weekend picnic. J. E. Lousley and his family had gone to the Chilterns in May 1947 with botanizing strictly relegated to second place. But, as he put it himself, 'I selected our stopping places on the chalk with some care, and naturally wandered off to see what I could find. To my delight I stumbled on the orchid just coming into flower.' No wonder one of his friends remarked that the find was less pure luck than 'inspired serendipity'! But the disarming casualness of this note is only in part due to Ted Lousley's modesty. He knew about the rapacity of orchid

The military orchid at one of its two remaining British sites. Suffolk, May

Yellow horned-poppy, named from its striking curved seed pods. North Norfolk, July

collectors, and never made the exact location of his find public. It was not until the 1960s that his colony – or quite possibly another one in the same area – was rediscovered in a remote beechwood in Buckinghamshire. This time local naturalists took steps to ensure that it would not vanish again because of any human agency by setting an electric fence around it. There were rumours of round-the-clock watches, and of a warden who carried a shotgun with his sandwiches . . . Souldiers Cullions was about to be restored to the public, but on rather different terms from those it had enjoyed in Gerard's day.

When the press were finally told about the return of this prodigal to an idyllic woodland glade only 50 miles from London, they knew they had a story. For the *Mirror*'s photographer it meant 'a pledge of secrecy, a rendezvous in a car park off a lonely country road . . . A long walk, an electrified fence, a last few careful steps . . .' And there, 'The Beauty That Must Blossom in Secret', the headline in the shadows. More people must have seen the rather smudgy black and white picture of *Orchis militaris* the following morning than had seen the live plant in its whole history in this country. Yet it seemed a far cry from the 'little hillock in the corner of a ploughed field' and the chance of finding it for yourself on a spring picnic.

The military orchid's journey into obscurity, and then back into rather sensational limelight inside a maximum security enclosure, could be a metaphor for the fate of all our wild plants. As agriculture becomes more and more specialized, so does the landscape which supports it. Woods and meadows are used as little more than factories for timber and grass. Commons which once supported half a dozen rights of grazing and gathering and a range of habitats and flowers which reflected this diversity, have been turned into arable prairies. There is not much *room* left for wild plants, and they are not just dwindling in numbers but passing out of our lives.

Even the bare statistics are chilling. Twenty native species have become extinct in the last 200 years (twelve this century). The beautiful lady's-slipper orchid is down to a single site, and the monkey orchid to three. Another 150 species are restricted to less than five locations. One in twenty of our wild flowers have been driven to or over the edge since the seventeenth century.* The reasons for this decline scarcely need repeating: 4000-year-old downland has been ploughed up for kale and medieval woodland sprayed with defoliants. You will be hard put today to find cornflowers in a cornfield or wood anemones in a spruce plantation. Some plants, like the cranberry, have been so thoroughly drained from land and memory that it comes as a surprise to learn that they were once common British natives.

But perhaps none of this matters. One frequently hears the argument that, because so much of our landscape is man-made, its wild vegetation is also 'artificial' and we should be prepared to accept its current drastic alterations as the logical extension of this ancient order. If we want 'wild' flowers we should grow them in parks and gardens, not expect them to be supported by a landscape with which they no longer have any 'natural' connection.

It can be a persuasive argument, but its assumption that the plant-scape is entirely man-made is as dubious as the earlier notion that it is entirely natural. However much we may reduce and rearrange them, wild plants are living organisms and have an independent existence that can never be entirely suppressed. They have been our partners in the shaping of the countryside, not inanimate counters shunted about our draughtsmen's boards. The relationship between us has been a two-way affair and, if we have influenced their fortunes, they have left their trace on ours. They are a living record not just of soils and seasons, but of five millennia of human activity.

What seems to me as great a danger as losing this species or that is that we may lose touch with these meanings and with the sense of intimacy with plants that is built deep into our culture. I wonder when the last common (meaning ordinary or

---

* Recent figures (1987) show that this attrition is continuing, especially at a local level. Many counties have already lost a tenth of their native species.

popular) name was added to the list of tens of thousands that have been coined anonymously for our plants over the centuries, and of which Souldiers Cullions was just one vivid example. And when it ceases to be familiar, does even an abundant plant cease to be 'common', in the other sense of 'well-known, shared'?

I don't think it any accident that the word 'common' has such richly ambiguous meanings in the world of natural growth. Plants have always been human familiars, and they are hedged about with associations of place and history. It is these physical and cultural settings that are as important as the plant itself. Field poppies, for instance, commonly pop up in gardens, and are safe enough from extinction there. But those little patches in the herbaceous border are no substitute for the sight of a mass of scarlet in the ripening corn. Nor are bluebells in a wood the same as bluebells in a vase, though we may visit the one in order to fill the other.

It is associations of this kind which have turned out to be the subject of this book. When Tony and I began work on it back in 1973 its aims had been more straightforward. We had wanted, first and foremost, to produce a collection of photographs which showed wild flowers growing in their natural settings. They were to be in the strongest possible contrast to the abstracted, flashlit portraits that make up the mainstream of plant photography. We both feel that these present an unhappily over-scientific view of flowers, and have a good deal in common with the narrow spirit of Victorian collecting. The text, similarly, would attempt to provide a comprehensive history of our flora in terms of the landscape in which it grew and the human beings who had shaped it.

In the event my plans for the text proved absurdly over-ambitious, and I opted for a more modest and more variegated commentary. What saved me from exposing the full breadth of my arrogance was the wonderful capacity of wild flowers to distract one from the job in hand. Our subjects refused utterly to be tidied away in a pre-arranged historical filing system. They sprouted wild, unexpected, exuberant stories. They would stun us with shows of pure unmediated colour one moment, then almost vanish as physical entities, so dense were the histories in which they proved to be entangled. They would appear where they

*Parish flowers – cowslips spared in a
Cambridgeshire churchyard, May*

had no business to be, and defy days of searching in places where they were supposed to have been abundant for centuries. Plants we saw vilified as pests in twentieth-century weedkiller catalogues turned up in more reverential settings in accounts of pre-Christian religious rituals. We found wild plants figuring large in Anglo-Saxon boundary charters, in Tudor medicinal potions, in Victorian children's stories and in the carefully planned 'rough' corners of modern suburban gardens.

Our furthest expedition was to look for rare alpine flowers in the north-west Highlands, an exploration of 300-million-year-old rocks that ought perhaps to have been conducted with reverence and a proper sense of history. As it happened our lamentable climbing – guided, as a last resort, by an altimeter – turned it into a comic treasure hunt. Yet 500 miles nearer home, in the medieval woods and villages of East Anglia, the sense of the past in the patterning of plants on the land was inescapable. We found trees that had mapped out the anatomy of settlements for more than five centuries, and whose persistence on those sites had as much to do with genetics as human affection.

Many of the plants we found had strong human attachments of one kind or another: the herbs which lingered on in the ruins of old monasteries; the arable weeds on chalky fields in the Chilterns that had probably been there since the Iron Age. There were mysterious alliances, too. Why were wild daffodils so abundant in just one small corner of Gloucestershire, and mistletoe a few miles further west in Hereford? Mistletoe was one of many plants whose history proved to be a remarkable record of magic and superstition. There were others whose role in the landscape was quite plainly as economically useful plants. Yet it was impossible to look at flowers like the tiny field forget-me-not and respond with anything other than simple uncomplicated delight.

The names of our wild plants are, in themselves, a record of the immense variety of their meanings. Some have as many as 100 local names across the British Isles. You can read from them the aspects of flowers that have touched people's affections: a time of flowering, a likeness, a tenacious attachment to a particular habitat. So there are primroses and lady's slippers and wood anemones. There are also flowers loved so much that they have been taken out of their native patches into gardens, and some that have moved the other way – over the wall and into the wild.

Tony and I ranged over the whole of the British Isles on our researches, from the extraordinary limestone pavements in County Clare to the more familiar downland chalks in Sussex, from Pembrokeshire cliffs to wheatfields in Skye. Yet whilst I was writing the text I found I was being continually drawn closer to home, not just to the literal territory of my own parish, but to the personal meanings that plants held for me – and, by implication, towards the personal meanings they held for other people.

As for my own parish – and it will appear many times in the following pages – even at the most public level its bounds seem to be mapped out by plants. They are, in the truest sense, landmarks – signs on, and of, the land. The town lies along a narrow river valley in the Chilterns, near the border between Hertfordshire and Buckinghamshire. On its north side the chalk hills are capped with an expanse of flinty clays and sands. It is poor soil here, commonland for the most part, and marked out unmistakably by its ragged cover of gorse and bracken and birch scrub. Up till the beginning of this century the fern was cut for cattle litter and the gorse for fuel. (The furze was apparently valued as much for its blazing vanilla-scented flowers as its burning branches, and there is a tradition in our parish – as in many others all over the south of England – that it was on *our* common that Linnaeus knelt down and wept for joy.)

On the south side of the valley, there is another landmark, an ancient droveway, 5 miles long, that skirts and overlooks the town, linking four common greens (once used for grazing) and the site of a curative oak, and lined with hedges that contain a total of twenty-eight different species of native shrub and tree. And on steep slopes throughout the parish there are beechwoods, some in large plantations, some abandoned remnants of what may have been the original woodland on these southerly chalklands. Two of these are called 'the Bluebell Wood' –

Mountain avens has probably been continuously present in this country for a million years. Widespread after the retreat of the glaciers, it is now confined chiefly to mountainous regions. County Clare, May

Marsh marigold, another glacial survivor, still widespread in damp places. Inverness-shire, May

confusingly, perhaps, and not marked as such on the map. But anyone who lives within half a mile of either will know them by this name. It is a functional description, in no more need of qualification than 'the ironmongers'.

There are other botanical monuments: a single colony of our Easter anemone, the Pasque flower, which has bloomed sporadically on the same site for more than 150 years; and a string of roadside grazing meadows so dense with buttercups that if you drive past on a sunny day in May you must screw up your eyes against the glare. More personal shrines are a particular patch of celandines on a canal bank, whose opening has come to signify the beginning of spring for me; and, not a hundred yards away, a clump of the first flower I bothered to learn by its Latin name, *Impatiens capensis*, the orange balsam. That word *Impatiens*! It was the first indication I had that scientific names might actually *mean* something.

Wild flowers play these kinds of role in all our lives, generating loyalties which are often private and sentimental, but which taken together do, I think, express our vestigial feelings about ourselves as biological creatures, still responsive to a sense of territory and the movement of the seasons. They are echoes of the time when we were all involved with the plant world in a more literal and direct sense. But, as I have said, *The Flowering of Britain* is not an argument or a history so much as a series of variations on a theme. Both photographs and text can be looked on as reflections inspired by particular plants and plant-scapes, and as such are glimpses not just of an external landscape but of the culture of flowers which we still carry with us in our folk memories.

PLANTS IN THE LANDSCAPE: A POTTED HISTORY

There is no 'natural' point to begin the story of the British flora, no abrupt clean sweep or fresh start. Each turn in the plot has been connected inextricably with what went before and what followed after. The nearest thing to a climacteric we will find is the moment about 5500 BC when the rising sea level separated Britain from the continent, which is at least definitive in a geographical sense. But as a botanical point it is too late, for by then our complement of plants and plant communities was virtually complete. If we go to another extreme, to the Eocene period 60 million years ago, say, we have gone back far beyond anything recognizably home-grown. The wishbone-shaped land mass that was to become Britain was cloaked with tropical evergreen forest of the kind that grows today in south-east Asia. Remains of identifiable plants from this period have been uncovered near the Isle of Sheppey, and three-quarters of them have living relations in the Malayan islands. In the upland areas there were magnolia woods of a type now typical of the temperate reaches of the Himalayas. There are virtually no signs at this time of anything resembling the contemporary European flora.

The most turbulent period of transition between this exotic flora and the plants that grow wild with us today was brought about by the arrival of the Ice Age. The glaciers began to move towards Britain about 2 million years ago, at the end of a long period of cooling that enabled many more familiar plants to migrate south into Britain. Pollen deposits dated to this period suggest a forest in which oak, hornbeam, elm and birch were mixed with more northerly (and no longer native) conifers like hemlock and spruce. And as the climate deteriorated further and the tree cover began to break up, so plants favouring more open conditions flourished and spread, including the various members of the heather family that were to become such a characteristic feature of our flora.

But the vast ice sheet which had formed in Scandinavia scoured much of Britain clear of these plants. Four times it advanced and four times it retreated. At its furthest extent it covered England as far south as the Bristol Channel, to a depth of 3000 feet in places. No Thames flowed through the Wiltshire water meadows. Oxford looked out over frozen tundra that stretched, unbroken by any sea, into the heart of Europe. During the coldest phases of the great freeze, Britain's flora was reduced to the few score species that could survive in these spartan conditions –

OVERLEAF: *Scots pine in Ross-shire. A remnant of the Caledonian Forest that once covered much of the central Highlands*

mostly grasses, sedges and herbs which now have an arctic or alpine distribution, and low-lying, frost-tolerant shrubs like juniper and the arctic willows and birches.

But during the periods when the ice retreated (known as 'interglacials' – one of which we are probably living in at present) many more species would migrate back from unfrozen parts of southern Europe where conditions had been favourable enough for them to survive. The famous collection of plant remains found in 600,000-year-old deposits along the Cromer coast again contains familiar tree species, including oak, beech, hazel, hornbeam and yew. But their most fascinating evidence is of a group of plants whose presence at this time is crucial to understanding the fortunes of our flora when humans became the dominant force in shaping the landscape.

At no time during any of the warm interglacials would all the dry land have been carpeted with trees. Whilst the ice was retreating, for instance, there would have been great expanses of open ground – glacial screes, crumbling cliffs, the gravelly edges of new rivers formed as the meltwaters poured away to the sea. The conditions must have been a little like those on a modern building site. And, sure enough, turning up in the deposits from this time are the remains of plants that we find on just such patches of disturbed ground today. Chickweed, sorrel, knotgrass were all here, poised to become the bane of farmers and gardeners half a million years before they had begun their work.

When the glaciers began their most recent retreat about 14,000 years ago, there would again have been an increasing area of open ground. Great volumes of rock which had been pushed south by the glaciers and shattered by frosts were strewn even further by the meltwaters. Because of the thinness of the plant cover and the scouring action of the ice there was very little humus, though silt was beginning to accumulate in the new river valleys scooped out by the glaciers. In the south of England, where chalk and limestone rocks had been laid down 100 million years before by the slow precipitation of the skeletons of myriads of tiny sea creatures, the hills were covered with only the thinnest film of earth. Rank plants that depended on rich soil found it hard to flourish and there was room and opportunity for almost any species of slow and modest growth. So, as the climate continued to improve, a great variety of species were able to move in from the south. Bellflowers, bedstraws, willow-herbs and meadow-rues came up from central Europe and the Mediterranean. A few species, like strawberry-tree and a number of scarce heathers, probably migrated north along the western European seaboard, which at this time was still an unbroken coastal strip stretching from Portugal to Ireland. And, as soil began to accumulate and temperatures rise still further, so the trees arrived, birch at first (a great pioneer then as now) followed by pine, hazel, and the first oaks and elms.

In those halcyon days around 7000 BC, before the climax forest was fully established, the whole of England must have resembled an artfully landscaped wild garden. In the dry alpine summers, on open ground in which there was still no great competition for space, plants we now think of as being confined to highly specialized habitats grew amicably side by side. Rock-roses scrambled not just over the chalk but any patch of dry ground. Cornflowers bloomed on the so far cornless wastes of central East Anglia. Sea-pinks grew far inland and mountain avens at sea level. The exquisite cobalt-blue sprays of jacob's ladder that are now only to be found in a few isolated spots in the Pennines cropped up all over England. Scattered about amongst these brilliant rockeries were groves of birch and aspen and juniper and, further south, more substantial blocks of woodland.

There are still a few places (the Burren in County Clare is the supreme example – see pages 35 and 158) where we can catch a glimpse of what this pre-Boreal Eden may have looked like. Because of freak combinations of climate and geology, these sites were never completely covered by forest, and the extraordinary plant collages that were characteristic of post-glacial Britain were able to survive. But by about 6000 BC most of the lowlands were blanketed by woodland. The only areas clear of trees were marshes, bogs, steep slopes and mountainous reaches above 2500 feet. For the plants of open habitats, at least, the easy times were over. Increasingly they were edged out to small enclaves, niches where their particular life-styles gave them an advantage over other species. Frost-tolerant species retreated to the mountains and those that could put up with salt spray clung on along the coast.

Although the coming of the trees undoubtedly produced a darker and more monotonous landscape, it would be wrong to imagine the climax forest as some undifferentiated and impenetrable mantle, a continuous thicket where one stretch was much the same as any other. In the warm south, small-leaved lime was as common as oak. In the cooler Scottish Highlands, pines were able to hold their own against the more sun-hungry deciduous species. Yew grew on the chalk and alder in the waterlogged ground by wide rivers. None of these species or communities were exclusive to any area, but were interwoven in a continuously changing fabric, broken by natural clearings created by fire and flood, and studded with smaller numbers of more modest trees – members of the *Sorbus* family, for example, like rowan and wild service. In the south-east, hornbeam and beech were beginning to return, though this time they did not seem able to penetrate the dominant cover of oak, lime and wych-elm in any quantity (and were not to do so until humans began to make substantial inroads into the natural forest cover). Stone Age people were already busy in the landscape, but they were nomadic hunter-gatherers at this stage, and made little lasting impression on the flora. They would open up clearings for their temporary settlements by a mixture of burning and rough hacking, but they rarely stayed on a single site for any length of time, and when they moved on the forest soon closed up again.

A remarkable picture of the woodland mix at this time – and, implicitly, of human activity in it – is given in an eighteenth-century account of a buried forest uncovered during the drainage of Hatfield Chase, an area of fenland south of the Humber:

> In the soil of all, or most of the said 180,000 acres of land, of which 90,000 were drained, even in the bottom of the river Ouse . . . are found vast multitudes of the roots and trunks of trees of all sizes, great and small, that this island either formerly did, or at present does produce; as firs, oaks, birch, beech, yew, thorn, willow, ash, etc., the roots of all or most of which stand in the

A sundew 'meadow' near Ambleside, Cumbria. Sundews would have been early colonizers of the acid bogs formed during the 'Atlantic' period

soil in their natural positions, as thick as ever they could grow, and the trunks of most of them lie by their proper roots . . . a 3d part of all being pitch trees, or firs. . . . It is very observable, and manifestly evident, that many of these trees of all sorts have been burnt, but especially the pitch or fir trees, some quite through, and some all on one side; some have been found chopped, squared, some bored through, others half split with large wooden wedges and stones in them and broken axe heads, somewhat like sacrificing axes in shape, and all this at such places and such depths, as never could be opened since the destruction of the forest, till the time of the drainage.

The reasons why this entire landscape had been fossilized in peat had to do with a change in climate that set in after 6000 BC. Rainfall increased, and there was a substantial rise in sea level, presumably as a result of the great volume of water released as the more northerly glaciers continued to thaw. In upland Britain the rainfall was very high. On high plateaux and badly drained valleys, peat began to form as plant remains accumulated and were prevented from decaying properly because of increasingly acidic conditions in the waterlogged soil. Many lowland areas were inundated by the sea, which submerged the woodland and created areas of marsh and fen. This was especially marked in the east of England, since the whole land mass of Britain was also 'warping' at this time, rising in the north-west and sinking in the south-east.

The most significant event in this long period of dampening occurred quite early. About 5500 BC the sea broke through the land bridge that separated the Straits of Dover and the North Sea, and Britain became an island. It's quite likely that this led to an even more pronounced 'oceanity' in the climate (this whole period from 5500 to 3000 BC is referred to as 'the Atlantic'); but its chief botanical importance was that it marked the last occasion on which most plant species could colonize Britain from the south by purely natural means. The flowering plants that were established at this moment – about 1500 species – are conventionally regarded as our 'native' flora, and almost all subsequent additions can be attributed to deliberate or accidental introductions. This critical break in plant communication routes is one reason why the wild flora of Britain is so much poorer than that, say, of France (which has about 6000 native species).

There were more changes in the climate over the next 5000 years. About 3000 BC the warm and wet Atlantic era gave way to a period of warm, dry 'continental' conditions, which 2000 years later was superseded in its turn by a cold, wet spell. Yet in terms of their impact on our flora these changes were dwarfed by one crucial development: the beginning of settled agriculture round about 3500 BC. A new breed of farmers had recently arrived in these islands from the Mediterranean. They had crossed the Channel with their domesticated animals and cereals (which had mixed in with them seeds of the weeds that were to become the first artificially introduced plants to our islands), and a culture whose technology and social framework was radically different from that of the Stone Age residents. These were pastoralists of a kind, too, and we should not underestimate their achievements. But what was different about the new colonists' approach to agriculture was its foundation in more fixed and settled communities, and as a result the changes they introduced to the landscape had a degree of permanence not seen before. When an area of forest was cleared for arable crops or for grazing animals, it remained cleared, and the first 'artificial' heathlands and grasslands were created. The neolithic farmers moved into areas where the soil was thin and the trees easily cleared – the chalklands of Wessex, Salisbury Plain, the East Anglian Breckland. It is quite possible that there are fragments in all these areas that have had a continuous history as grassland as far back as this period.

There is also evidence that woodland was being *managed* as well as cleared. One of the most characteristic features of the pollen record is the dramatic reduction in the proportion of elm which occurs around 3500 BC. It is doubtful if this is a consequence of the general process of forest clearance, as it is not matched by a *proportional* decline in the pollen of other trees. It is more likely that it represents the harvesting of elm boughs from living trees. This prevented them flowering and producing pollen, but in most cases actually prolonged the life of the tree itself. The young foliage was needed for one of the colonists' most radical innovations – the fattening of cattle in enclosed stalls. Elm was a favourite browse plant, and there can be little doubt that it would have been selectively cropped to provide fodder. In harvesting the young branches – high enough in the trees to be above the browse line – the neolithic farmers created the first pollards, one of the earliest and most ingenious examples of a 'continuous yield system'. And to judge from the unnaturally straight poles excavated from 'corduroy' trackways, in Somerset, for instance, they had also begun a rough and ready form of coppicing (the regular cutting of trees back to ground level, so that they send out sheaves of new, straight shoots from the base).

By the time the Celts had arrived (*c.* 800 BC) with their Iron Age culture, all the basic components of what we understand as the rural landscape were already established. A good deal of the forest had been either modified, or cleared and replaced by more open habitats. There were pastured grasslands on the hills, heaths on more acid soils, hay meadows in the valleys, arable fields up to a mile across, scrub where these had been abandoned or grazing reduced, and a great variety of wilder land, from coppice woodland to sedge fens. What is striking is the way this essentially artificial landscape recapitulated the open conditions that had existed quite naturally 6000 years before. So plant species that had been greatly reduced during the period of climax forest were able to spread out again, with marshland and river-bank species colonizing the meadows, those from chalk cliffs moving on to the downs and so on.

And this is the point where we can begin to take up the story in more detail, for all the changes that were to occur in the plant-scape over the next 2000 years were really just variations on this basic pattern. The Romans, for instance, introduced from the continent a number of plants (later to become naturalized) that might well have made their own way here but for the opening of the Channel. The Normans, addicted to the chase, protected considerable areas of poor land from premature cultivation in their Royal Forests. Saxon farmers added thousands of miles of hedgerow, ditch and lane. Although there was a consistent movement over these two millennia away from natural woodland towards open agricultural land, this happened gradually, and the new habitats (except, of course, for arable

*The rich plant mix of old chalk
grassland on the Sussex downs: wild
thyme, lady's bedstraw, squinancywort,
self-heal. The turf on parts of these
downs may date from neolithic times*

land) were not normally cultivated but simply maintained and harvested as they stood. The changes thus presented an opportunity, once again, for a variety of plants from different kinds of open habitat to prosper. It was not really until the beginnings of industrial agriculture in the nineteenth century, when a pattern of repeated cultivation, replanting and chemical treatment became the rule for every kind of habitat from woodland to pasture, that the retreat of our flowers began. If we can compare the impact of traditional farming on our flora to that of a glacier frozen in a state of retreat, modern agriculture behaves like a glacier in permanent, animated advance, and increasingly our contemporary flora is dominated by the limited number of adaptable species that can survive such conditions of turmoil.

PART TWO

Wood

Living in a country where only 9 per cent of the land is covered with trees – and most of that in remote areas of the uplands – we are not great connoisseurs of woodland. We are fond enough of trees (just so long as they are not too densely packed together), and in spring and autumn, when there is a sense of change and colour, we even begin to enjoy our local copses and spinneys. But darker seasons, bigger woods, *forests* . . . they are another matter. They are too disorderly, too full of shadow and decay for most modern tastes. Our ideal wood is green and snug, light and roomy, with a few secret glades and dark corners to add a hint of romance, but not so big that we cannot find our way out. Louis MacNeice, in a poem about the Dorset copses he knew as a child, talks about their 'dark but gentle ambush', their best of both worlds:

> . . . whatever its name
> Each wood is the mystery and the recurring shock
> Of its dark coolness is a foreign voice.
>
> Yet in using the word tame my father was maybe right,
> These woods are not the Forest; each is moored
> To a village somewhere near. If not of to-day
> They are not like the wilds of Mayo, they are assured
> Of their place by men; reprieved from the neolithic night
> By gamekeepers or Herrick's girls at play.
>
> And always we walk out again. The patch
> Of sky at the end of the path grows and discloses
> An ordered open air long ruled by dyke and fence . . .
>
> from 'Woods'

Perhaps it is because we are no longer involved in the use of woods (as our not-so-remote ancestors were) that we imagine such compact groves to be entirely human creations; and that we think of woods not so much as living structures as collections of individual trees and flowers.

The dark and flowerless prospects of Britain's new forests: Forestry Commission plantation. Redesdale, Northumberland

If one believes most of our woods are modern creations, there is something very seductive about the idea that there may be, somewhere, some patch of primeval forest just as it was 7000 years ago, untouched by human hand. There is not of course. Even if there are a handful of woods in impenetrable upland ravines that have never seen an axe or been invaded by browsing cattle, they have not escaped the insidious effects of the twentieth century's atmosphere, which is full of toxic chemicals (and equally alien seeds) that were unknown even 100 years ago. Nor can we consider such fragments – however 'unaltered' they may be – apart from the overall woodland cover. The very fact that they are now reduced and isolated relics means that their flora is likely to be undergoing a slow process of impoverishment. If a plant species is lost for any reason there is simply nowhere for it to recolonize from.

Various woods have, from time to time, been popularly claimed as pristine relics of the old forest, but none of these claims can stand up to examination. Wistman's Wood on Dartmoor, with its famous dwarf oaks, has been shown by aerial photography to owe a good deal of its current area to growth in the last fifty years. The remnants of the great Scots pine forests that once covered the central Highlands have been repeatedly felled and interplanted. Staverton Park in Suffolk is an ancient deer park, whose oaks were pollarded as recently as 250 years ago. The New Forest is only a forest in the traditional legalistic sense of an area reserved for the king's chase. It contains (and probably has done for 4000 years) much more heath than woodland, and the character of its tree cover has been irrevocably changed by centuries of grazing and lopping.

None of this makes these woods any the less fascinating. The closer you look at them, the more absurd it becomes to bother about whether or not they are untouched relics of the Wildwood. What strikes you again and again is not the absence of change but the evidence of *continuity* and it is in this, after all, rather than changelessness, that the identity of living things lies. Much of Wistman's Wood may indeed be comparatively young, but its new oaks have sprung directly from the twisted, elfin trees that form the heart of the wood, which in their turn are the lineal descendants of oaks that grew on the lower reaches of Dartmoor in the Stone Age. You will not find trees like these in a planted oakwood, nor the woodrushes and wood sorrel that are spreading out beneath them. Nor do new pine plantations – even in the Scottish Highlands – carry the luxuriant carpet of juniper and lady's-tresses orchids that carpet even the most hacked-about remnants of the Old Forest of Caledon.

It is in how this continuity was preserved in some woods and lost in others that the fascination of our woodland flora lies, rather than in the search for some mythically virgin fragment of the primeval forest. We may not have a great number of old woods left in Britain, but they are an astonishingly rich and diverse collection. No two are exactly alike, and the flowers that grow in each one raise their own intriguing questions.

Why are bluebells so rarely found covering the ground in new plantations, as they do so freely and frequently in most local copses? Why is the true oxlip – abundant on the continent – confined to a curiously tight cluster of clayland coppices in central East Anglia? Why does bird cherry grow as a common shrub amongst northern hills and vanish almost entirely as you move south, only to reappear here and there in Norfolk, one of Britain's flattest counties? What combination of circumstances – not the absence of change, we can be certain – has managed to 'hold' a few areas of woodland in Britain to the plant communities they must have carried thousands of years ago: the juniper woods of Upper Teesdale (vintage 8000 BC), Taynish Wood in Kintyre (5000 BC), the limewoods of Lincolnshire (3000 BC)?

Perhaps the least altered woods in the British Isles are the hazel groves on the Burren in County Clare, where climate and grazing have preserved a woodland type that was present in Britain maybe 9000 years ago. I say more about the flowers of this remarkable area of glaciated limestone pavement later. As far as the woods themselves are concerned, it seems as if the comparative lack of soil on the flat rocks has made it difficult for timber trees to grow in conventional ways. Although the rainfall is high this far west, it drains away quickly through the broken slabs of limestone, and is of little use to the plants. What trees there are mostly creep about in the cracks between the rocks, where conditions are moister and some humus tends to collect. Those that are inclined to grow higher are grazed back by cattle and feral goats.

But hazel seems perfectly happy in these deprived conditions. It has a shallow root system and tolerates browsing, putting up new stems from the base. The Burren hazels are so durable that it is difficult to tell the ancient trees from the merely old, yet each wood has its own peculiar character. Some are so dense that you must crawl about on your hands and knees to get through them. Others are growing in such impoverished ground that they never reach more than 3 or 4 feet in height, and you can experience the comic sensation of meandering, like Gulliver, through a forest that comes up no higher than your chest. It is in these exceptionally stunted woods on the barest rocks that you may have the equally disorientating experience of seeing alpine flowers – spring gentian and mountain avens – growing under the 'trees'. In the taller copses it is as damp and muggy as a rain forest, in contrast to the sharp heat reflected off the bare limestone outside. And here you will find a multitude of more conventional woodland flowers revelling in the warmth and shelter – bluebell, early purple orchid, bugle, stitchwort, primrose. They do not grow in dense masses as they do in the rich leaf moulds of full-sized woods; there is just not enough soil to go round for that. They are scattered in ones and twos wherever there is a niche or crack in the rock, growing through the carpet of moss which swathes every rock and rotting branch. They are surprisingly beautiful seen in these solitary clumps, quite renewed if you are used to them in kaleidoscopic masses, and thoroughly in scale with these Lilliputian forests.

The spring flowers of the Burren woodlets raise the compulsive question that recurs whenever we consider the cultural history of our flora. Why these flowers, growing here, in just this way?

Early purple orchids in a Burren hazel grove. May

SNOWDROPS AND BLUEBELLS

Because its pollen deteriorates so quickly, we know less about the ground flora of the prehistoric woods than we do about their trees. Yet there is no reason to suppose it differed greatly from that which grows in long-established woodland today. When peat layers dating from the neolithic period were excavated from the bottom of old Buckenham Mere in Norfolk, there, amongst the pollen of oak and hazel and elm, were the remains of a spring carpet that included dog's mercury, bluebell and stitchwort.

Yet one familiar woodland plant of which no trace has been found in prehistoric deposits is the snowdrop. You would think it would have been perfectly at home in post-glacial Britain. It has leaf-tips specially hardened for pushing through frozen ground, and hangs its flowers on stalks elastic and flexible enough to ride out winter gales. It would be pleasant to think of them breaking through the last traces of glacial frost, just as they often do through the snow in our modern woods. But in most of the parks and copses in which it is found, the snowdrop is quite patently a garden escape. And paradoxically, it is only in the West Country, where the winters are often mild and muggy, that it begins to behave like a truly wild flower and crop up in damp woods and along river banks, well away from habitation.

It may seem pedantic to quibble about the snowdrop's origins. Whether it is an escape from cultivation or some kind of climatic anomaly, it is plainly thoroughly at home as a wilding, and in some woods the first new flowering of the year. Yet the story of a plant's movement from country to country, from wood to garden and back again, is not just its own biography. It is also a record of our feelings towards it.

The snowdrop grows in indisputably wild habitats in woods and damp meadows across most of Europe, though its densest populations have a definite alpine distribution. Yet the first non-garden records in Britain were as late as the 1770s, when it was found in Gloucestershire and Worcestershire. *The Oxford*

English Dictionary finds no reference to the word before the late seventeenth century. Go back another 50 years, and in the first edition of Gerard's massive *Herbal* there is no mention of the plant by name at all. Yet there, on page 120, after the tulips, is an unmistakable portrait of the frail, drooping, three-petalled flower, under the heading '*Leucoium bulbosum praecox minus*: Timely flouring bulbous Violet'. Now I suspect that is altogether too mannered and cumbersome a name for a plant that was at large in our woods and village lanes, and the *Herbal* states explicitly that Gerard knew snowdrops only as plants of metropolitan gardens. But in the 1633 edition, revised by Thomas Johnson, there is a note that 'some call them also Snow drops'. It may be that this is just a translation of some of the European names (the German *Schneetropfen*, for instance). But it may also be a clue that the plant was by then loose in the countryside, and attracting the eyes of a generation more imaginative in their naming of plants than our own.

Gerard gives more circumstantial evidence about the plant's origins when he talks about its scent. 'Touching the faculties of these bulbous Violets we have nothing to say . . . only that they are maintained and cherished in gardens for the beautie and rareness of the floures, and sweetnesse of their smell.' Walter de la Mare, moved more by poetic fancy, I suspect, than a keen sense of smell, once wrote to a friend that they have 'a faint fresh earthy scent suggestive, indeed, of snow itself'. To most noses snowdrops have anything but the musty scent of snow. They are faint, certainly; ethereal, if you must find a snowy, ephemeral comparison. But Gerard was right; the smell is unmistakably sweet and nectarous (and much the same as you find in other pallid early flowerers like the winter heliotrope), and there can be little doubt that it represents a bait for equally early bees.

Snowdrops are so classically elegant and simple in outline that we rarely bother to examine them closely. But almost every detail of the blossom suggests that they are adapted to attract pollinating insects. The whole flower opens more widely on warm days, the better to admit any insects that may be about. And inside the corolla, whose edge is ringed and scalloped like a medieval cuff, there are green, nectar-bearing striations, which act as trails down to the pollen clusters.

So the snowdrop emerges as something of a paradox. It was not recognized as a wild plant in this country until the eighteenth century. It grows naturally only in the south-west of Britain and appears to be designed for the kind of insect attention it can rarely receive in our climate. Yet everything else about it suggests a plant admirably adapted to the vagaries of British winters. Perhaps the answer is that it is on the very edge of its range here, happier where the springs are longer and warmer, but well prepared for late frosts nonetheless. This would accord with the plant's distribution on the continent, and perhaps explain why the wild stock in this country is confined to sheltered woods in the mild south-west.

Yet though it may not easily set seed in this country, its bulbs once planted will spread very readily, and some of the colonies on old estates are huge and ancient. In the tangled copses at the back of the medieval Grey Friars priory at Dunwich, they range right up to the remains of the thirteenth-century skirting wall. So many of the best colonies seem to be on the sites of old monasteries. Did the monks plant them out so that they could gather the pure white flowers for Candlemas Day, the Feast of the Purification of the Virgin which falls on 2 February?

Snowdrops came into most of our woods almost by an act of will. More than any other garden plant they are planted haphazardly, in dark and untended corners; dared, almost, to break bounds, and loved most of all when they do, edging in scattered clumps away into the shade. Settled like this they will map for centuries the contours of old gardens – and old festivals. I have only been able to trace one record of a 'wild' colony for my own parish. De Crespigny, in his *New London Flora* (1877), mentions '*Galanthus nivalis*; meadows, Bourne End Mill.' I know the mill well. It has long been a motel, but when I discovered de Crespigny's reference I used to scan the grounds each spring for signs of this old colony. I had no luck until one precociously warm February afternoon in 1977. It was the kind of day that would make a snowdrop gape, and along the edges of the derelict mill leat I could just see a sheet of the wide-open flowers, lying like a layer of frost deep in

Snowdrops. Hertfordshire, February.

the grass. They were a fortnight late for Candlemas, but it was their local centenary, in a way, and I think they could be forgiven.

If snowdrops are newcomers to most of our woods, bluebells have been there for almost as long as we have records of the ground flora. They are true woodland plants, tolerant of shade, growing in both dense scrub and open forest, under oak and hazel and beech, from Cornish hedgebanks to Caithness birchwoods. They have a preference for old, undisturbed woods, but they will spread from these into new deciduous plantations, and then again linger on some sites long after the original woodland cover has disappeared. Sometimes you will see drifts of bluebells hanging incongruously on railway embankments and bracken-covered hillsides, relics of the time these sites were covered by trees.

Yet their persistence in open surroundings is a sign that bluebells, like so many other woodland plants, do not *need* shade. They can tolerate it better than many other species, but the association of dense bluebell colonies with old woodland is as much due to the stability of these sites as to the degree of darkness in them. Indeed, the thinning of a bluebell wood is often followed, the next spring, by a great increase in blossoming because of the extra sunlight the plants have soaked up. In those areas where bluebells will grow only in woods, it is probably their need for moisture and warmth that stops them spreading. In the damp and mild climate of western Britain, for instance, they will thrive almost anywhere, even on cliffs overhanging the sea that have probably never seen a tree, let alone a wood. But in East Anglia, where the rainfall can be as low as 17 inches a year, they are virtually confined to ancient, undisturbed woodland. Yet even that is oversimplifying their needs. They can seem so magnanimous where they do grow, flooding every gully and mound, reappearing year after year, never retreating. But perhaps that is what we want to see. In a minutely detailed study of the ground flora of one medieval wood in Cambridgeshire, it was found that bluebells only really flourish – only drench the ground in the uncompromising way we always picture – in situations where the drainage is exactly right. In especially damp areas they tend to grow best on raised mounds. On well-drained slopes where dog's mercury is able to flourish, they keep to the hollows.

It is this broken patchwork of blue that gives spring woodland floors that sparkled, submerged glow, like light reflected and scattered from water. I know one wood where bluebells grow in an austere and glittering backcloth of whites – wild garlic, woodruff, wood anemone, stitchwort – as if a winter-flowering meadow had been unfurled under the trees. In other woods bluebells bloom (and never for a moment clash) with the orange-flecked 'weasel-snouts' of yellow archangel, with early purple orchids, and with the dimmer blue of bugle. On the Chilterns, bluebells often grow under beech, especially where these have been planted amongst oak and hornbeam on the more clayey soils. It's a chance association, but a perfect match. The bluebells and beech leaves open together in the first week of May, and when sunlight filters through the translucent young leaves and shines back from the blue flowers and grey trunks, it is as if the woods have been dusted with phosphorescence.

These quilted blocks of colour in springtime woods have their own special quality. But there is no sight in our whole island flora which can match bluebells *en masse* – unmixed, undiluted, clear up to the trees. It is a uniquely British spectacle, denied to most Europeans because of the bluebell's liking for damp westerly woods. And this was how Gerard Manley Hopkins loved the flower, 'wash wet like lakes', and which moved him to write some of the most evocative plant descriptions in the language. In his journal for 1871 he talks of bluebells 'in falls of sky-colour washing the brows and slacks of the ground with vein-blue'. Again, in May 1873, 'Bluebells in Hodder Wood, all hanging their heads one way. I caught as well as I could while my companions talked, the Greek rightness of their beauty, the lovely – what people call – "gracious" bidding one to another or all one way,

OVERLEAF: *Bluebells in old oakwood. Dorset, May*

the level or stage or shire of colour they make hanging in the air a foot above the grass. . . .'

It is this 'shire of colour', shifting and lapping in the breeze, that makes bluebell picking so popular – and, to my mind, so pointless. Taken away from that wash of colour and the animation of the breeze, bluebells are lifeless and leggy, scarcely distinguishable from the plastic imitations that are so often made of them. Still, they are an abundant plant, and a resilient one, and if the chance to continue gathering 'juicy and jostling shocks' makes people more determined to defend their bluebell woods against the bulldozers, perhaps it is a custom worth tolerating.

In any case, experiments have shown that it is not so much the picking that harms the plant, as the damage done to the leaves by the pickers' feet. Bluebells are in leaf from mid-February to June, and as the woodland canopy grows more dense during the summer the leaves wither away. They are crucially important to the plant for the few months they are open to the sun, for they have to manufacture enough food to see it through the rest of the year. During the dark months of summer and the cold of winter, bluebells (and many other spring-flowering woodland plants) go to ground in a kind of siege economy, storing their energy resources in bulbs and tuberous root systems. It is in the ground itself that the identity of a wood lies. Both its past history and its future potential are locked away beneath the soil, guaranteeing the thread of continuity against what may happen above. We have to remember this if we are to understand the remarkable groupings of plants that grow in our woods, and how a sea of bluebells can survive in an embattled farming landscape inside an island of wood that may itself have been repeatedly felled and beaten about. Every old wood is a unique community that has absorbed the changes that have occurred throughout its history, and yet kept something of its character intact.

THE WAILING WOOD

Wayland Wood, in south Norfolk, is one such ancient community, and parts of it may have an unbroken ancestry back to the primeval forest. It is not a particularly imposing place from the outside, tucked up close to the main Thetford road, low-slung and unprepossessing, and easy to pass by if you are concentrating on the awkward bends that follow its western boundary. You will see no great trees and a good deal of what looks, at a glance, like young scrub. But Wayland has credentials which suggest that it is a very old wood indeed. There is a detailed map dating from 1723. There are records going back to the fourteenth century, when the wood came into the possession of the de Grey family and was an important local source of wood and timber. 300 years earlier Domesday records woodland for the Hundred of *Wanelund*, a word derived from the Old Norse *lundr*, meaning a sacred grove. There was in all likelihood an important, named, wood here as early as the ninth century.

Wayland Wood's most celebrated claim to antiquity (though not its oldest) is that it is believed to be the setting of the Babes in the Wood, the only well-known British folk tale to feature woodland in a star role. No one is sure when the incidents recorded in the story happened, or indeed whether they have any exact historical parallels. But it's generally accepted that the tale was inspired by the misdemeanours of a genuine wicked uncle in the de Grey family. It was already a legend by the early sixteenth century and was commemorated in a carved wooden fireplace in neighbouring Griston Hall. There is a superstition in the area that the wails of the doomed children can still be heard at midnight, though it would be hard to say whether this grew out of the original legend, or from a corruption of the ancient name of the wood. Either way, Wailing Wood is a fitting title for such a lonely relic of an old order.

Wayland is known as the one remaining site in Norfolk for the yellow star-of-bethlehem, and it was the chance of finding this scarce plant that first prompted me to visit it. I must confess it was not so much the blooms themselves that intrigued me – they are modest in the extreme – as the rather poignant account of the only occasion this century on which *Gagea lutea* had been recorded for my home county of Hertfordshire. This featured another babe in a wood, a girl from Ware Grammar School, who, our *County Flora* despondently reports, 'found it in "Broxbourne Woods" but could not recall the exact location. Its status in the county is uncertain.'

One reason behind this uncertainty is yellow star-of-bethlehem's erratic flowering habits. On the rare occasions it does bother to put out blooms they appear early, and you must be in the woods some time in April to be sure of seeing them. Very few tree species are in leaf at this time, but Wayland, in early spring, is anything but colourless. Much of the understorey is decked out with the bright green leaf sprays of bird cherry, a shrub that in the southern half of England is virtually confined to ancient woods in Norfolk. There are sheaves of bluebell leaves, the broader speckled blades of early purple orchid, and here and there a few primroses in flower. But Wayland's speciality at this time of year is its show of wood anemones, many of which are in a shade of delicate rose-purple that I have only seen elsewhere in such quantities in Devon. Where they grow directly under the bird cherry, the contrast is strikingly stark, of the kind you see in Japanese gardens: the pale purple petals, as sharp-cut as paper flowers, the moss on the bare earth, the pale shine on the underside of the cherry leaves, the dark trunks behind.

These little bowers have a self-contained glimmer, but outside it is hard not to feel some sympathy for the Babes' plight. Many of the rides are narrow and overgrown, and there are few conspicuous trees or glades to act as landmarks. And the closer you look at it, the more cryptic and complex the wood's structure appears. On three sides it is bordered by deep ditches, and there are a number of curious earthworks actually inside the wood. There are groves of aspen and alder on damp patches near the main ride. And though much of the rest of the wood is dominated by oak and hazel, on the eastern flank there is a block of more mixed forest, with sycamore, wych-elm and huge, multiple-stemmed ash stools. There are also some unusually uniform patches of hornbeam. You are in the realms of

Wood anemone, a speciality of Wayland, here growing through newly cut coppice in Suffolk, April

historical speculation here. Is this area evidence that part of the original wood had once been cleared, for arable perhaps, only to be subsequently abandoned and given back to the trees? The quantities of ash, a species which rapidly colonizes open areas, suggests that it might be. So does the presence of hornbeam, which is really beyond its natural range this far north. Had it perhaps been deliberately planted in the wood? Hornbeam is a naturally gregarious tree and can form pure stands quite naturally, but it was also frequently planted in similar formations for the sake of the valuable firewood it provided, and it can be hard to tell natural and planted groves apart.

I have, I am rather thankful to say, found no tidy answers to these questions, not yet succeeded in tracking down Wayland's star-of-bethlehem. But I did make one special discovery on my first visit. Just as I was about to leave the wood, I came across a man cutting small hazel wands near the main track. We began talking, and he told me his story of the later years of the Wailing Wood.

He was in his late sixties, and had been working for himself in the wood for more than forty years. Each winter he used to purchase the right to coppice so many acres of underwood. (His exact words, I think, were that he 'bought a few acres of the wood', and this phrasing cut so strangely across our conventional notions of land ownership and use that I did not understand him at first.) He had made hurdles from the hazel and broom-handles from the ash. The rest he bundled up for firewood, except for the thin wands of the bird-cherry, which, he assured me, made perfect chrysanthemum stakes. During the last war the whole wood had come close to being cleared – 'taken in' – to make way for an aerodrome. But it was the years immediately after that had been the hard time for Wayland. He told me how the bulldozers had come in to take out the big standard oaks, and how their caterpillar tracks had crushed and killed many of the underwood stools. Now the wood had been bought as a nature reserve by the Norfolk Naturalists' Trust and, though he was worried about his own future in it, he had already noticed hints of a quiet revival, a new liveliness. He pointed to where the early purple orchids – 'cuckoo flowers', he called them – were pushing through along the newly-cleared ride. He was reduced to cutting pea-sticks, but the wood looked set to prosper.

These old woods, weather-beaten, hard-worked, spun about with legend and history, each one stocked with its own exclusive cargo of flowers, are life-rafts out of the past. You do not need to spend very long amongst the mounds and stumps and very singular plants of Wayland to be persuaded that there may have been a wood on this site for 8000 years.

It is the great age and complex history of such communities that helps to explain why so many familiar woodland plants can be so abundant in them, and yet not occur at all in new plantations. We can imagine them jostling for position over the centuries, the drifts of shade-tolerant, spring-flowering perennials gaining ground during the long periods of dark, lapping each other's boundaries, retreating when the wood was disturbed and laid open for quick-growing weeds, then slowly returning as the canopy closed over again: wood anemone, wood sorrel, wood spurge, wood goldilocks, bluebell and dog's mercury in oakwoods, woodruff and sanicle in beechwoods, lily-of-the-valley in some ashwoods. Old, natural, comparatively undisturbed woodland is the aboriginal home of these species, and if it is destroyed to make way for a new plantation, they are unlikely to survive. Most of them cannot even cross a few hundred yards of cultivated land from an old wood to a new. And so we find the typical species of plantations – bramble, bracken, rosebay and the like – having more in common with the opportunist inhabitants of hedgebanks and waste ground than with those of old woods.

It is the cutting of the links between one wood and another that is partly responsible for the distinctive and sometimes bizarre distribution of many of our scarcer woodland plants. Solomon's seal, for example, grows in woods in north Kent, south Wales, a small area of Westmorland, a good deal of Wiltshire and Hampshire, and, indisputably wild, almost nowhere else. I know the plant well from gardens, but it was only recently that I recognized it in a properly wild setting in Hampshire. I had been tempted into a wood whose name – Thedden Copse – summoned like a bell from the dark ages. I was about 200 yards into the wood when I noticed a clump of the plant, underhung with its buttery white bellflowers, like rows of teats. I could hardly have missed it, as it was in a patch of recently cut hazel and surrounded by plants – early purple orchid, woodruff, town-hall-clock – I was very familiar with. It was the walk back that was embarrassing, as I realized that the path I had climbed up was lined with the flower almost as far as my car. There was some excuse for my blindness in the habit of the plant, which can make it hard to see in a well-leafed wood: it grows tall and bowed, with the same slope as a thin sapling, and holds its shelves of grey-green leaves parallel to the ground, obscuring the flowers and only catching the light occasionally. But my failure had as much to do with my expectations, which were based on the flowers that grow in more easterly woods, where solomon's seal is rarely found.

The evergreen stinking hellebore also grows in Hampshire woods, and in a scatter of other areas on the southern chalk and limestone. You can still see it in the hanging beechwood at Selborne – exactly where Gilbert White recorded it 200 years ago, noting that the local women 'give the leaves powdered to children troubled with worms'. Its deciduous cousin, green hellebore or bearsfoot, is more widespread, but also favours steep slopes on the chalk. Yet there are also considerable clumps of it in the damp bottom of a ravine wood on the Old Red Sandstone in Herefordshire. (The wood is called, in a delightful semantic chaos, Hill Hole Dingle, and the owner's wife refers to the hellebores as 'those green buttercups' – an excellent and botanically exact description.)

The names of woods, and of the places near them, can be clues to their history and to the location of scarce woodland plants. These are usually conspicuous or useful trees and shrubs (though there is a 'wild garlic wood' in the specifications of a piece of land in Berkshire granted by King Edmund to Bishop Aelfric in 944 AD). In the Weald of Kent chequer trees – a vernacular term for the wild service tree – can still be found close by Chequertree farms, Chequertree houses and Chequers

Bird's nest orchid. A species without its own chlorophyll, which feeds from decaying plant remains in the soil, and is largely confined to old woods where the humus is deep and damp. Hampshire, June

pubs. This association between chequer trees and chequer place names occurs nowhere else in Britain.

Similarly Box Hill (Surrey), Boxley (Kent) and Boxwell (Gloucestershire) still have wild box groves near them, and are all places whose names can be traced back to before the twelfth century. There are a score of other 'box' places in the south of England; the fact that there are no longer any box trees associated with them is a direct result of the ruthless exploitation of this tree for its valuable wood.

Woodland clearance is also the most likely explanation for the odd distribution of the may lily, *Maianthemum bifolium*, which, though it has no place names to announce its presence, is even more thinly scattered. It once grew in acid woods in at least ten counties in Britain, and had a celebrated site in Ken Wood, Hampstead. Now it is known as a probable native from just four localities – in Durham, in Northumberland, and in two isolated woods in East Anglia. One of these is the lime copse in Lincolnshire where the Rev. Keble Martin sketched a specimen in June 1931. Our native cyclamen is even more drastically reduced, embattled in two or three copses in the Kentish Weald. The mysterious ghost orchid, which lives off dead vegetable matter in the deep humus of undisturbed woods, can scarcely be said to have even one regular station. Although it has cropped up in half a dozen places this century – in Herefordshire, Oxfordshire and Buckinghamshire – it is so slow-growing and sensitive to climate that it may only flower once every twenty years.

Another species of unpredictable appearance, though more widespread distribution, is the caper spurge, *Euphorbia lathyrus*. These days it is most often seen as an ornamental garden plant, though it used occasionally to be cultivated for food in the mistaken belief that its green fruits were the capers of commerce, *Capparis spinosa*. (It was a bad mistake: the spurge's fruits are a drastic purgative.) Seed from cultivated plants, old and new, is no doubt the source of the specimens that crop up from time to time on waste ground. But caper spurge is regarded as a native in old coppice woodland on calcareous soil. On these sites it has the habit of vanishing for years, only to reappear (from dormant seed, presumably) when an area of the wood is opened up to the light by coppicing or felling. Crested cow-wheat, whose purple flowers are stacked as elaborately as a Christmas table decoration, behaves in the same way in a few woods in eastern England.

In fact most shade-tolerant woodland flowers respond favourably to coppicing, demonstrating just how little connection there is between the cutting of wood and the clearance of woodland. They flower more profusely and spread more freely, and it is likely that the intermingled sheets of spring-flowering species that we associate with old woods are partly a result of this once widespread system of management. In Hayley Wood, Cambridgeshire, the flowering of oxlips can increase seven-fold and of violets up to forty-fold in the second spring after coppicing. In some damp areas of the Bradfield woods, Suffolk (where there is also a unique coppice mixture of alder and white willow) there are almost unbroken colonies of ramsons nearly an acre in extent, and you can understand how a 'wild garlic wood' could have been regarded as a landmark in the tenth century. In the summer immediately following coppicing the newly cut compartments carry a dense growth of ranker, light-loving species, such as meadowsweet, marsh thistle and water avens.

The most distinctive plant in the Bradfield woods, and the one with perhaps the most intriguing distribution of any woodland species in Britain, is the true oxlip, *Primula elatior*. Although this can be exceptionally prolific where it does occur (there used to be 4 million plants in Hayley Wood's 122 acres) it is almost exclusively confined to ancient coppice woods on an oval-shaped area of boulder-clay covering west Suffolk, north Essex and south Cambridgeshire. So exact is the relationship that in this area you can identify ancient woods by the presence of oxlips, or conversely be sure of oxlips by locating an ancient wood. I once went on an oxlip hunt in this patch of East Anglia, seeing how many sites I could find in woods that looked, from their names and outlines on the map, as if they might have ancient origins. It was only a day's outing, covering maybe half a dozen different woods, but I struck lucky in every one of them. I found oxlips in full flower in Easter Wood (it was exactly a week after Good Friday), though they were sharing it with browsing cattle. They spilled out over the verge from the thin deciduous edge of a roadside clump called Haws Wood, the rest of which had vanished under a pall of conifers. They were scattered about a kidney-shaped manorial copse close to, and named after, Dovedenhall, and in one short stretch of a hedgerow that joined the wood to the road. This clump was something of a curiosity, as oxlips are poor colonizers and cannot usually jump any distance from their parent wood. (I solved the mystery some years later when I saw a map of the area produced in 1783. At this time, there was a wing of the wood jutting out as far as the road. This seemed to have been grubbed out round about 1800, leaving the hedgebank as a relic.) The most splendid display was in another wood 'moored to a village somewhere near', which I visited largely because it lay, tantalizingly unnamed on the map, at the end of a mile-long track past a moated medieval farmhouse. (It turned out to be Bulls Wood, a reserve managed by the Suffolk Trust for Nature Conservation.)

The loyalty of oxlips to old woods in this part of the country is matched for strangeness by the fact that they were not recognized as a distinct species until the 1840s. Traditionally the name 'oxlip' referred to the much more widespread (though less numerous) hybrid between the primrose and the cowslip, *Primula veris* × *vulgaris*. This is almost certainly the oxlip that Shakespeare refers to on the 'bank where the wild thyme blows', and again in the *Winter's Tale*, where Perdita distinguishes it by the epithet 'bold'. (The habit of the flowers, splayed and upright at the end of the stalk in the hybrid, is what marks it out most conspicuously from the true oxlip, whose smaller flowers droop more closely together, all facing the same way.) Gerard's 'Oxlips or Paigles' are also the hybrid, and he makes no mention at all of *P. elatior*. Sowerby's *English Botany*, written in 1798, carries a picture of the true oxlip (labelled as *P. elatior*), but rejects it as a separate species:

> In describing the Primrose, we expressed a suspicion that the Oxlip might be a variety of that rather than the Cowslip, or possibly a hybrid between the two. We are still much inclined to the latter opinion and that it has originated from a Primrose impregnated by a Cowslip; its external habit, the contraction

Oxlips, Primula elatior. *Bradfield Woods, Suffolk, April*

towards the middle of the leaf, and the umbellate flower-stalk indicating (according to Linnaeus's ingenious idea) the father, while the blossom itself, in form, colour and scent, most resembles its mother. . . .

It is hard for us to understand why the countless millions of true oxlips growing so distinctively and so regularly in the woods and meadows of East Anglia were not seen as a separate species. Perhaps they were by the locals. Perhaps it was only those botanists who were familiar with the *Primulas'* promiscuous and variable habits who assumed oxlips were merely a particularly compact regional form of the cowslip-primrose hybrid.

It was not until the 1840s that two Essex botanists, George Gibson and Henry Doubleday, finally established the oxlip's true credentials. It was Doubleday's observations of the plants round Great Bardfield, in particular, that clinched the issue: 'They cannot be hybrids, for the primrose does not exist in the parish and these oxlips grow by the thousand in the meadow and in moist woody places adjoining: in one instance a meadow of about two acres is entirely covered by them, being a mass of yellow bloom.' *Primula elatior* was subsequently named the Bardfield oxlip to distinguish it from the hybrid.

Essex continued to be the prime area for investigations into the plant's curious distribution. It was from his work in the county that R. Miller Christy put forward his often repeated (though, we now realize, misguided) theory that oxlips were in a state of accelerating decline as a result of being 'hybridised out of existence' by the more 'aggressive' primrose. Since the Second World War, attention has been concentrated on the geological properties of the East Anglian boulder-clay deposits, and it looks as if these may indeed have some special physical qualities which could explain the oxlip's attachment to this area. Certainly no other factor correlates so closely with their distribution. Despite far-reaching changes in land-use, for instance, the overall scatter of oxlip 'zones' today remains identical with that mapped by Miller Christy at the beginning of the century. Even the almost total loss from meadowland (a habitat in which they are still common on the continent) can be explained by the wholesale conversion of old meadows to ploughed leys since the war, and oxlips have invariably survived in adjacent, undisturbed woodland.

And that, I thought, was probably all there was to learn about the oxlip's territorial loyalties – until I began finding colonies of it in a group of woods on the Hertfordshire–Buckinghamshire border, 40 miles south-west of its traditional range. I had come across the first patches one April in a little spinney known locally as Long Wood (more because of its minuscule width than its length, I suspect) strung out along the edge of the main track and looking as securely at home as the primroses that grew nearby. I did not know then that the species had been overlooked by botanists for centuries, and it did not cross my mind that I might have done the same. This was one of my home woods, these plants were strangers, and therefore, I presumed, they must have been sneaked in deliberately, behind my back. The fact that Long Wood, despite its diminutive size, was a very rich fragment of ancient wood spared from the plough because of its slope, did not change my mind. It was too far from the accepted oxlip area. It was not even on boulder-clay, but on a thin clay over pure chalk. And such an attractive plant, so close to a footpath. . . . It did seem to be asking too much of coincidence.

But two springs later (and rather more knowledgeable about the species) I found much larger numbers in a 40 acre coppice wood half a mile away, then in two more small woods nearby (one of which was, improbably, a mixed beech-wood carpeted with coralroot). It turned out that oxlips were present in every wood in an area covering about a square mile, and altogether I found more than 200 separate plants.

The conventional attitude towards outcrops of a species way outside its usual range is that they are planted unless proven wild. Yet the more colonies that turned up, the more preposterous the idea of some deliberate introduction seemed. Nor had I ever heard of the successful naturalization of oxlips in a wild setting. There was a small colony in the relatively cosseted setting of a churchyard in Staffordshire, but every attempted introduction to a woodland setting had, to my knowledge, quickly died out. Yet all my local colonies were flourishing in the highly competitive company of species like bluebell, woodruff, yellow archangel and goldilocks that are characteristic of long-established woods in the Chilterns.

The only other explanation was that they were an 'outlier' population, an isolated relic of a time when oxlips had a more widespread distribution. (There is one such outlier in a boggy meadow at Dickleburgh in Norfolk, though this is only about 15 miles north of the conventional area.) There was some support for this possibility in the first edition Ordnance Survey map (dating from about 1820). All the woods in which the oxlips grew were featured on this map, and at that time formed part of a suite of eleven, whose eccentric outlines and close jigsaw formation suggested they had been carved out of what was once a larger block of continuous woodland.

I have watched these colonies for some years now, and they show no signs of real advance or retreat, though they do better some seasons than others, and young seedlings are constantly replacing ageing plants. However they came here in the first place, they are plainly well enough established to prove that oxlips do not need to be rooted in East Anglian boulder-clay to prosper in the wild. Whether they are stranded relics of a time when oxlips were more widespread in south-east England, or the legacy of some diligent (and extremely secretive) botanical evangelist, they are living proof of how tolerant and rewarding plants can be if they are only allowed a little stability.*

SPRING MESSENGERS AND SWALLOW-HERBS

The majority of woodland plants come into flower and leaf early in the spring, to catch what light they can before the canopy closes up (which is partly why they

---

* The oxlips continue to survive, and to pose tantalizing questions. I have now traced an earlier map of the area (Dury and Andrews, 1766) and on this the existence of a single, continuous stretch of woodland is quite clear. But I have also heard of a wartime vicar with a passion for planting out wild flowers in improbable places . . .

*Spring flowers in a Dorset hedgebank
in April: celandine, dog violet, primrose*

often bloom so much more profusely after coppicing). Their response to the gradual lengthening of the hours of daylight and to rising temperatures is so regular that it is possible to plot the advance of spring across Britain in terms of their first opening. The scale is based on 'isophenes', which are lines joining the points where the average first flowering of a given species occurs on the same day. They are very discriminating contours. A flower which blooms in mid-April in the sheltered combes of south Dorset will be opening simultaneously in the warm Atlantic breezes on the Pembrokeshire coast and in humid pockets in the New Forest. Yet on the exposed scarp of the South Downs, only 20 miles to the east of the Forest, it may not be open for another fortnight, and it will be a full three weeks before it blossoms in the bleak wastes of Dartmoor (whose isophenes pass also through Snowdonia and the Inner Hebrides). Using these measures botanists have calculated that spring moves north across flat ground at roughly 2 miles per hour – strolling pace, in fact, which means that you can indulge in the pleasant fantasy of following it on foot, the guest behind the unrolling carpet.

The precocious blooming of our woodland flowers is reflected in their names. Primrose is *prima rosa*, the 'first rose' of the year. The wild daffodil is the Lent lily. In Somerset, wood anemones are simultaneously Candlemas bells and cuckoo flowers, which rather generously stretches their flowering period. (In other parts of the West Country 'cuckoo flower' can mean bluebell, red campion or lady's smock, *Cardamine pratensis*. In East Anglia, as we have seen, it refers to the early purple orchid.) The names of plants – and particularly their ancient vernacular names – are amongst the most revealing evidence we have of how they have figured in people's lives. And none more so than the compendium of titles collected by the celandine, a flower whose names trace the journey which many adaptable plants made out of the Wildwood and into the light – not just of the cleared forest, but of a new consciouness of their power as talismans and healers.

Celandine – lesser celandine in official botanical English, pilewort in unofficial, *Ranunculus ficaria* in Latin, golden stars in Somerset (and that is as good a straight description as you will find), and, in Dorset, spring messenger, the one and only

British flower to be so confidently christened. I am no Dorseter, but celandine is my spring messenger too, and I would cheerfully march across the isophenes after it. It is rarely the first flower to open in the spring, being invariably beaten by the snowdrop (though that whiteness somehow signals the end of winter more than a new beginning), and often by waste-ground coltsfoot. But those shiny, butter-yellow stars are, for me, the first fine-weather flowers, opening wider as the sun shines and the days lengthen, optimistically bridging the last of winter and the beginning of summer as they must have done 10,000 years ago.

So much for 'spring messenger'. But what about that curious tag, 'celandine'? It is a very ancient naming, which can be traced back to the Greek word *chelidon*, a swallow. Celandines were thus swallow-herbs (they are still swallow-worts in America), perhaps, as the sixteenth-century herbalist Henry Lyte imagined, because they 'beginneth to springe and to flowre at the comming of the swallows'. Plain enough. But most celandines are out long before the arrival of the swallows. In the latter half of the eighteenth century Gilbert White worked out that the average first flowering round his Hampshire village of Selborne was 21 February. A whole century later, one of our Hertfordshire botanists, John Hopkinson, gives precisely the same date for the period between 1876 and 1886. Another hundred years on and this is still the week celandines appear across much of southern England. These are average dates, of course, and a long winter or a mild spell in January can shift a local date weeks either way. In mild winters I could, I remember, usually find a bud sufficiently advanced to be persuaded into bloom by a sunray lamp in time for St Valentine's Day – a spring messenger of another kind!

Perhaps the echo in the flower's name is due to something less literal than a coincidence between blossoming and a bird's arrival. Perhaps celandine was seen as a kind of vegetable swallow, the flower that, like the bird, signalled the arrival of summer, whatever the cautious might say (and there are floral false alarms, too).

But plant names that have survived as long as the celandine's rarely have a single root. As the American biologist Lewis Thomas has said, the oldest, most persistent words are 'membranous, packed with layers of meaning, like one-word poem. . . .'

He also said that 'the great thing about human language is that it prevents us from sticking to the matter in hand'. Which ought to remind us that the name celandine is indeed attached to another matter – another plant altogether. This is *Chelidonium majus*, the greater celandine, a member of the poppy family only remotely related to the *Ranunculacae*. Yet notice the *chelidon* root, the swallow connection, in its specific scientific name. It is a very peculiar coincidence. The greater celandine is in all probability a southern European introduction to this country, with four-petalled, custard-yellow flowers carried on rather tall, hairy stems, and bearing no physical resemblance whatever to the lesser. It is hardly possible that botanical writers who, by the sixteenth century, were capable of distinguishing most of our obscurely different native buttercups, could be using the same name for the two plants because they could not tell them apart.

Gerard, for one, was plainly embarrassed by the confusions perpetuated by the 'old writers', though out of a sense of deference (first named is best named is still part of botanical protocol) continued to use the same name for the two plants. Nevertheless he stresses that they are 'much differing in forme and figure', and, though he has nothing to say about the origins of lesser celandine's name, he is quite plain about the source of *Chelidonium majus*'s swallowness:

> It is called celandine, not because it then first springeth at the coming of the swallows, or dieth when they goe away: for as we have said, it may be found all the year, but because some hold opinion, that with this herb the dammes [female swallows] restore sight to their young ones when their eies be out: which things are vain and false.

This is a quite different way of looking at the origins of the name, the possibility that it may be *functional*. And though Gerard derides the superstition, he is not averse to recommending the juice of the plant for the same purpose in human eyes, for 'it clenseth and consumeth away slimie things that cleave about the ball of the eie'. (He makes no mention of the most elaborated version of the legend, which speculated that the reason swallows had problems with their eyes was because they spent the winter hibernating in the mud at the bottom of ponds.)

Herb robert – the medieval herbalists' Herba Sancti Ruperti *– amongst germander speedwell.*
Gloucestershire, May

We are not much nearer a satisfactory explanation of lesser celandine's swallow tag; and no clearer at all about why two such dissimilar plants should share a common name. Yet in exploring the roots of that name we have already moved from looking at flowers as indicators of the seasons to their role in early herbal medicine. This is curious territory and, though far removed from diagnosis and treatment as we understand them, does tell us a good deal about the symbolic importance which was once attached to plants.

Gerard's prescription for eyewash was in fact as ancient and dubious as the swallow legend itself. And, though it had obvious roots in magic and pagan beliefs, it was for centuries supported by Christian physicians. Probably the first reference by an English writer to its use comes in the seventeenth book of *De Proprietatibus Rerum*, written by Bartholomaeus Anglicus in the middle of the thirteenth century. Not a great deal is known about Bartholomew. He was born in England, but spent much of his life in France as a Franciscan friar. He quickly became one of the most brilliant and popular philosophers of his day, and the section *De Herbis* in his monumental theological work must stand as the first truly popular herbal of the middle ages. Its clarity, vividness, and obvious love for and intimacy with plants, marks it out from almost everything written previously – and a great deal since. In 1398 *De Proprietatibus Rerum* was sympathetically translated by the Cornishman John de Trevisa (later the vicar of Berkeley).

Bartholomew had much to say about 'medycynall herbes', including celandine: 'Celidonia is an herbe w^t yelowe floures, the frute smorcheth them that it towchyth. And hyghte Celidonia for it spryngeth, other [or] blomyth, in the comynge of swalowes. . . . It hyst celidonia for it helpith swalowes birdes yf their eyen be hurte other blynde. . . .' So two centuries before Gerard, there is already a double-meaning. Yet by his reference to the 'frute' which 'smorcheth them that it towchyth', Bartholomew is plainly talking about greater celandine, whose acrid orange juice is so corrosive that it was once used to cauterize warts (which may give you some idea of its effects upon the eye).

If we delve still further back into Christian herbal medicine there is no doubt that the greater celandine has prior title to the name. On the thirteenth-century shrine to St Frideswide in Oxford Cathedral, there is a carving of what is almost certainly *Chelidonium majus*. At a quick glance you might think it just a conventional leafy motif – it has that formal, fingered style so popular in church ornamentation – until you remember that St Frideswide, as well as being the patron saint of Oxford University, is also a benefactor of the blind. Given the eminence of the institution for which the good lady has responsibility, she has a very obscure biography. She seems to have been the daughter of a twelfth-century Mercian princess, and to have gone into hiding for three years to avoid an arranged marriage. Her unfortunate suitor subsequently went blind, and Frideswide, in an act of contrition, entered holy orders. Not long after, she summoned a holy well to spring up in the village of Binsey, just upriver from Oxford. Its waters apparently had miraculous powers, especially for stomach and, appropriately, eye troubles, and this seems to have been the reason for her sanctification. Pilgrims began visiting the site in the saint's lifetime, and by the seventeenth century the water from the well was selling at a guinea a bottle. The well is still there, half hidden at the bottom of some mossy steps behind the village church of St Margaret. When I visited this remote churchyard one May, I half hoped to find a greater celandine by the well, planted or grown of its own accord, for it likes nothing better than slightly disturbed ground, with its back against a stone. There was none of course; but I should have expected the little clump of *lesser* celandine that was growing at the top of the steps.

There is just one final chapter in this long story of mistaken identities. Lesser celandine was Wordsworth's favourite plant. Although he claims not to have recognized it for 'thirty years or more', he wrote three poems about it, and when he died it was proposed as the most fitting decoration for his tomb. But the flower on the monument in Grasmere is not the lesser celandine, but the greater. Did the sculptor genuinely mistake the plant, or think that the leaves of *Chelidonium majus* were more decorative? Or was he a latter-day herbal magician, who believed the power of this herb to be the greater?

Yet it's no surprise that such confusion should have arisen over the identity of plants, or that the church repeatedly found itself in the midst of the tangle. For the 1000-year period between the end of the Roman occupation and the beginnings of the Renaissance, the people of Britain lived in a state of extreme seclusion. Although we were invaded more than once, communications were very bad, and communities tended to remain isolated and self-sufficient.

It was these conditions – a relative absence of unsettling new ideas, and a deep-rooted connection between community and place – that helped reinforce that intense relationship with nature that is one of the most conspicuous features of early medieval culture. Plants, especially, were regarded with the greatest respect as potent and mysterious influences on human fortunes. By comparison with animals, whose lives could be understood in part as an echo of the lives of humans, their ways were invisible and inscrutable. They could afflict you with disease, and then, contrarily, cure you. They could appear by apparently spontaneous generation from the earth. The secrets of their growth and power were beyond any common understanding. It is no wonder that the middle ages saw the development of a philosophy towards plants that was partly religious, partly magical and in part an embryonic ecology.

It was this pervading sense of superstition and (to our eyes) ignorance that led to this whole era being summarily described as the 'dark ages'. Yet it is becoming increasingly clear that the darkest aspect of this period is our lack of understanding of it. For written evidence we are largely dependent on the manuscripts produced by the religious establishments. The monastic orders were the intellectual as well as the spiritual centres of the time, and were deeply involved in the culture of plants. They had their own gardens, and used herbs grown in them to minister to the sick. And being part of the increasingly cosmopolitan organization of Christianity they played a key role in the dispersion of useful plants around Europe and the near East.

There may have been British Christians, pure and simple, at this period, but for the most part they were men and women who had adapted to the eclectic beliefs of

Angular solomon's seal, Polygonum odoratum, *in the treacherous grikes of Hutton Roof Crags, Cumbria. Like its lowland cousin,* P. multiflorum, *it was used for bruises and broken bones and in these rocky parts was once known as vagabond's friend*

medieval society, and were as steeped in Celtic paganism and Saxon lore as in the articles of their adopted faith. The oldest surviving manuscript dealing with the uses of herbs, the Leech Book of Bald, dates from about 950 AD, and it would be hard to imagine a more striking example of this blending of outright magic with orthodox religious practice. It was written by a Saxon scribe (in the vernacular, not Latin) and lodged at the Abbey of Glastonbury for much of what remained of the middle ages. Here is a typical prescription against 'elf disease' using 'helenium' (almost certainly elecampane, *Inula helenium*, which had been brought to this country by the Romans):

> Go on Thursday evening when the sun is set where thou knowest the helenium stands, then sing the Benedicite and Pater Noster and a litany and stick thy knife into the wort, make it stick fast and go away; go again when day and night just divide; at the same period go first to church and cross thyself and commend thyself to God; then go in silence and, though anything soever of an awful sort or man meet thee, say not thou to him any word ere thou come to the wort which on the evening before thou markedst; then sing the Benedicite and the Pater Noster and a litany, delve up the wort, let the knife stick in it; go again as quickly as thou art able to church and let it lie under the altar with the knife; let it lie till the sun be up, wash it afterwards, and make into a drink with bishopwort [betony] and lichen off a crucifix; boil in milk thrice, thrice pour holy water upon it and sing over it the Pater Noster, the Credo and the Gloria in Excelsis Deo, and sing upon it a litany and score with a sword round about it on three sides a cross, and then after that let the man drink the wort; soon it will be well with him.

Reading spells like this, we have to remember that before the development of the scientific method and the idea of objective proof, adherence to ritual played much the same role as experimental testing does in our day. It was a way of clinging to order, a kind of validation. Effects were in the lap of the gods, or God; the most mortals could do was to go through an invocatory ceremony as precisely and reverently as possible. Hence the minutely detailed stipulations as to the order of devotions, the time and place of pickings, and the manner in which the herb was administered. Most important of all was getting the plant 'right'. This did not involve the kind of pragmatic search we might make (looking for a species which had proved itself effective, for instance) but identifying as accurately as possible the species which had been traditionally 'given' for a disease. To this end, the beleaguered monks and scholars of the medieval period looked back to the golden age of classical learning, and in particular to Dioscorides's *De Materia Medica*. This long and surprisingly sensible encyclopaedia was written by a Greek army doctor in the first century AD, and was the most important influence on the medicinal use of plants in Europe for the next 1500 years. Each successive generation of herbalists regarded their foremost duty as the correct identification and interpretation of the plants mentioned by Dioscorides. With no original to work from, they laboriously copied each other's manuscripts, perpetuating an accumulating forest of confusion and error. By the eleventh century, when the style of accompanying illustrations had reached a Byzantine pitch of abstraction, the manuscript herbals were all but useless as practical identification guides.

It was not really until the first stirrings of the Renaissance in the twelfth and thirteenth centuries that a few monks began to draw, from life, the plants they grew and used in their own gardens. (The most striking example from this period is the *Herbarium* prepared in the Abbey of Bury St Edmunds about 1120, whose vivid paintings of blackberries, clover and chamomile are more fresh and lifelike than anything that had been drawn in Britain before.)

But by and large it is the plants which survive on the sites of old monasteries rather than the written manuscripts that give us the best clues to the herbs that were in use in the middle ages. Many of these have persisted on the tops of tall walls and in neglected stony corners, even where the monastery itself is in ruins. Birthwort is perhaps the most fascinating of these old monastic relics, and one at least that medieval herbalists had correctly identified from *De Materia Medica*. Dioscorides had mentioned the belief that it was 'thought to help passing well women in child-bed', perhaps because of a fancied resemblance between its curious funnel-shaped flowers and a uterus. Birthwort would have been a

standard herb in the gardens of any abbey where the nuns had midwifery duties.*
It still survives in the ruins of the nunnery at Godstow near Oxford, and in the
grounds of the Benedictine Carrow Abbey in Norwich (next to that modern herbal
enterprise, Colman's Mustard works). Not so long ago it also grew at the Hospital
of St Cross in Winchester, an almshouse set up in the early twelfth century. Not far
away in Hampshire, there is winter savory, ploughman's-spikenard, marjoram and
clove pink on the walls of Beaulieu Abbey, and a recently reconstructed medieval
herb garden in the beds beneath. Another pink, *Dianthus plumarius* (used as a
heart tonic), survives on the ruins of the Cistercians' Fountains Abbey in Yorkshire.
Travel a short distance to the east and you can see what may be an accidental
occurrence rather than planted relic, but an ironic one nonetheless: herb
christopher, or baneberry, on the magnificent abbey at Rievaulx. Not even the
most inventive herbalist has ever dreamed up a useful application for this
poisonous member of the buttercup family. I like to think that it was a monk with a
wry sense of humour who named it after the saint who, though better known for
looking after travellers, is also the Christian patron of wizards.

But the most remarkable collection of monastic survivors is on the island of
Steep Holm in the Bristol Channel. This has greater celandine, henbane (a
hypnotic), caper spurge (the 'Catapuce' in Chaucer's *Nun's Priest's Tale*, employed
as a laxative), coriander, red valerian, wild peony, and, until recently, milk thistle
and wild leek. Steep Holm was probably a retreat of Gildas, a sixth-century monk
and historian from Glastonbury, and a community of Augustine Canons lived there
between 1166 and 1260. John Fowles believes that the Augustines may have been
deliberately exploiting the island's equable oceanic climate for the growing of
bulk supplies of Mediterranean herbs. Certainly almost all the surviving medicinal

---

* Recent research has confirmed that birthwort is active both in speeding up labour, and
as an abortifacient. The Oxford botanist the late E. P. Warburg was told by an ecclesi-
astical doctor that its presence at so many nunneries helped keep many a little sin
hidden.

Evergreen alkanet, introduced to this country as a dye plant (quite likely by monks) and naturalized here outside a Cotswold garden. May

plants on Steep Holm are of southern European origin. Even the wild leek, *Allium ampeloprasum*, may have been introduced here. Although it does grow apparently wild in a few places in south-west Britain, its main populations are in southern Europe and one fourteenth-century continental writer clearly felt that it was a necessary companion in chilly climes. Leeks, he wrote, 'clear up catarrh of the chest. . . . They cause hot blood and acute crisis of the bile. They are primarily indicated for cold temperaments, for old people, in Winter, and in the Northerly regions.'

Steep Holm has proved a magnetic attraction to botanists ever since William Turner, author of *A New Herball*, visited it in 1562. Yet its most celebrated plant, the wild peony, was not discovered until 1803. The island is the only site in Britain where this Mediterranean introduction survives in a wild setting, and the fact that its dramatic flowers – they are a luscious deep red, and up to 5 inches across – were apparently not noticed for 300 years, has made some wonder whether it might not have been brought over by later and more whimsical visitors than the Brethren of St Michael. (After all, even Gerard had apparently 'insinuated' the plant into Kent. 'I have been told,' his editor Thomas Johnson confided, 'that our Author himselfe planted the Peionie there, and afterwards seemed to finde it there by accident: and I do beleeve it was so, because none before or since have ever seen or heard of it growing wild since in any parte of this Kingdome.')

Yet the wild peony is only in flower for seven days – it could easily have been missed – and a twelfth-century herb garden is still the most plausible explanation for its presence on the island. There is abundant evidence that it was regarded as one of the most precious of all medicinal herbs, for diseases as diverse as jaundice and depression. Gerard's final prescription for the plant is for those suffering from a 'disease called *Ephialtes* or night Mare, which is as though a heavy burthen were laid upon them, and they oppressed therewith'.

The one ancient herb that has retained some of its magical associations into the twentieth century is mistletoe. It is the only plant still in wide, popular use as a charm, yet one of the very few whose uncompromising pagan ancestry was at no time accommodated by Christianity. Even today, there are few churches that will include it as part of their Christmas decoration.

Our mistletoe, *Viscum album*, is the one British representative of the *Loranthaceae*, most of whose members live out bizarre existences in the tops of tropical rain forests. Not that ours is a commonplace plant. It is an epiphyte, rooted eerily above the earth; an evergreen, shining white and yellow whilst most other plants are bare; a partial parasite that is green enough to manufacture its own sugars but which takes minerals from its host. No wonder that it has been revered since antiquity, that its milky berries, suggestively paired between the splayed leaves, were used as an aphrodisiac and fertility potion, and that, as the master parasite, the whole plant was believed capable of overcoming lesser 'excrescences' in the body and 'drawing forth thick humours from them'. Mistletoe was the supreme symbol of spontaneous generation and continuing life. It could break the trances of epileptics and guarantee the crop of the fruit trees it haunted. Wear it round your neck and it would keep witches at bay; ensure peace, open locks, divine treasure. Throughout the world the various species have been held in similar awe, and it was an exotic mistletoe after which Sir James Frazer titled his monumental study of comparative folklore *The Golden Bough*.

In Herefordshire and Worcestershire, the heart of mistletoe country, echoes of these beliefs persisted into the early years of this century. Mistletoe has a natural south-westerly distribution in Britain, but its concentration in the border counties also has something to do with the great numbers of orchards in the area. One nineteenth-century writer found it on more than a third of the apple trees in Herefordshire, and it may have been the constancy of this relationship that kept fragments of the old fertility rites alive. In Herefordshire the boughs were brought into the cottages and farmhouses on New Year's Eve, and allowed to hang there for the rest of the year, to ensure good luck and a heavy crop. In Worcestershire it came in with the rest of the Christmas greenery and was dressed with apples and ribbons. If a woman was kissed under it she had to remove one of the berries, and this could be repeated until all the berries were gone.

It is not easy to see why this local and decidedly pagan custom should have become such a popular pastime in the nation's sitting rooms. But the tradition may well have been sparked off by the eighteenth-century fascination with Druidism. Druids and mistletoe had always been linked, and many people had heard of Pliny's account of the cutting ceremonies, with their white-robed priests and golden sickles. But it was the passionate and fanciful writings of a Lincolnshire doctor called William Stukeley that turned Druid-following into a cult and mistletoe into a fashionable plant. Gardeners and botanists began patenting methods for propagating the plant by implanting its berries under bark. Quack doctors revived old remedies and fabricated new ones, and joined nostalgic antiquarians in a nationwide search for the mistletoe sanctified by the Druids as the most potent of all – that growing from an oak. In 1741 Philip Miller wrote in *The Gardener's Dictionary* that 'whenever a Branch of an Oak-tree hath any of these plants growing upon it, it is cut off and preserved by the Curious in their Collections of Natural Curiosities; and of these there are but few to be seen in England'.

So the plant spread out across the country, and a fertility ritual softened to a Christmas kiss. Herefordshire farmers, of course, relished this upsurge of interest in one of their orchard weeds, and it became a valuable secondary crop for fruit growers. Some no doubt used the developing techniques of incision and grafting to increase their wild stock. The country's 'Curious' naturalists also enjoyed the plant's new status. In the mid-nineteenth century the Woolhope Naturalists' Field Club regularly hunted for mistletoe oaks on their outings, though with none of the reverence of metropolitan Druidists. They seemed to have had a particularly sprightly time with one growing near Aymestrey on 24 May 1870, and in their *Transactions* for that year you can read of this respectable company (one-third of

In mistletoe country. Warwickshire, February

the 150 members were clerics) going through a gentle parody of the rites of an earlier priestly elite:

> The bunch of mistletoe in the oak was so large that it could be exceedingly well seen from the adjoining lane, notwithstanding the foliage of the tree, 'There's no mistake about it', said one gentleman, as if he thought there possibly might have been, its portrait and the description in last year's volume of the Club notwithstanding! A ladder had been placed against the tree, with the same thoughtful consideration to every detail that could add to the pleasure of the visitors that prevailed throughout the reception, and it was soon mounted. There was no white yearling bull with garlanded horns to sacrifice beneath the tree for the festivities, nor was there an Archdruid to cut the mistletoe with a golden sickle – indeed the Druidical programme was rather reversed on the present occasion – but anyway the mistletoe bunch was reached and gathered amidst three rounds of applause that were given by the assembled multitude below, and small sprays of 'the heaven born plant unpolluted by any touch of the earth' were distributed to the ladies present and to all others who wished for it.

A mistletoe oak is still an exciting find, though not so rare as was believed by the Woolhope botanists. (They knew of ten in England in the 1860s, though there were probably as many as this in the region of Epping Forest alone.) Being planted in the wild exclusively by birds wiping their beaks after feeding from the berries, mistletoe is commonest on rough-barked fruiting trees in which birds are likely to be busy anyway. And its parasitic manner of growth is probably what makes it favour soft-barked trees like poplar, willow and lime.

It is the mistletoe which breaks these rules, growing on ill-matched trees, in incongruous or pleasingly appropriate places, that makes mistletoe hunting such an agreeable pastime. A fuzzy clump in the dim heart of a hazel bush still has an enchanted look; and I would love to have seen the one found in a wild rose in Northamptonshire in 1712. The most aptly sited plants I know are in a lime by the entrance gate to the Botanic Gardens in Oxford. The most amorously tempting are just 100 yards away, where a bushel attached to a hawthorn branch overhangs the

Cherwell, a few feet above your head if you are sitting in a punt. The most mysteriously beautiful are in the long avenue of limes at Kentwell Hall in Suffolk. The trees were planted in 1678, and they are covered with fig-shaped galls produced by generations of mistletoe. On moonlit nights in winter the clumps glisten palely in the upper branches like balls of mist.

Yet it is unwise to treat mistletoe's magical history too frivolously. When Tony and I were looking for suitable clumps to photograph we spent a Valentine's Day amongst the colonies that abound on the limes in the Thames valley near Cookham (it ought to be, we felt, a propitious date to search for a plant with such romantic associations). We had reached a particularly idyllic field, full of fine trees and grazing cattle, and were debating the merits of a bunch above us, when I was butted, fiercely and unexpectedly, from behind. Twice I was sent sprawling before I was able to scramble to the safety of a hedge. With lips untouched but a very sore back, I risked a look back at the reincarnated Druidic bull that had committed this act of vengeance. It was, I hardly need to say, a Hereford. I am only thankful it did not have garlanded horns.

SIMPLES AND WILDINGS

Very few of the herbal 'simples' that survive in gardens have retained the ancient resonances of mistletoe. They have been reduced to ornaments for the most part, with only a name or a diluted superstition to remind us of their history. Rhubarb, for example, which we know as a vegetable (or do we think of it as a fruit?) was originally introduced to this country as a purgative. To judge by the numbers of laxatives they used the medievals were obsessed by constipation. The most drastic of the home-grown remedies were the shiny black berries of common buckthorn, which Henry Lyte described in 1578 as being suitable only for 'young and lusty people of the country, which do set more store of their money than their lives'. One wonders, then, what must have been the digestive problems of the poor monks of the Benedictine Abbey of St Albans that drove them to use such quantities. When the latrine pits of the abbey were excavated in the 1920s, great numbers of buckthorn seeds were found mixed up with fragments of the cloth which the monks used as lavatory paper. Most young people in the countryside, I fancy, would have preferred the gentler remedy offered by fairy flax, *Linum catharticum*, whose little white flowers and wiry stalks are so frequent in chalk grassland. (Thomas Johnson learned about and recorded its use after seeing bunches for sale on an apothecary's stall near the Hampshire downs.)

But in the large towns it was a different matter. The dissolution of the monasteries and the expansive, inquisitive mood of the seventeenth century combined to produce a new breed of secular herbalists, an odd mix of scientific dabblers, earnest gardeners, mystics and hustlers. Exotic remedies from overseas were bandied about, and all manner of bizarre systems flourished in a climate of opinion that would support almost anything 'rational' or progressive. The most notorious system was the Doctrine of Signatures, which, in a kind of modern formalization of old sympathetic magic, was based on the theory that all plants were stamped with some physical indication as to their purpose and use. The white veins of milk thistle 'signed' it as an aid for nursing mothers. Celandine's knobbly roots indicated its use in a salve for warts, boils and, especially, piles (hence 'pilewort'). The nodding flower heads of cowslips were to be given for 'the shaking palsy' and, by association, for any afflictions of the head. One remedy for faintness was sniffing the juice of the flowers through a quill.

Astrology was also popular and had its most zealous advocate in Nicholas Culpeper. From his shop in the East End, Mr Culpeper (guided, as he repeatedly insisted, by 'Mr Reason and Mr Experience') harangued his potential customers with arguments more outlandishly devious than anything which came out of the dark ages:

> They say a mouse is under the dominion of the Moon, and that is the reason they feed in the night; the house of the Moon is Cancer; rats are of the same nature with mice, but a little bigger; Mars receives his fall in Cancer, ergo,

Wild pansy. One of the wild precursors of a favourite garden plant. Ravenglass, Cumbria, June

Wormwood being an herb of Mars is a present remedy for the biting of rats and mice.

The English Physician Enlarged

Although the colourful nonsense of signaturism and astrology may have proved seductive to a public that had no more effective remedies (their emphasis on cryptically powerful ingredients and fabulous associations is very reminiscent of modern hard-sell advertising), it had no lasting impact on the fortunes of our wild flowers. Away from the influence of fashionable books, household medicine was an altogether more pragmatic business, guided as it always has been by trial and error, family custom, neighbourly recommendations, and by rumours of more distant and remarkable cures. That is not to say that superstition and a healthy respect for the local witch were not still strong influences. But they were increasingly tempered by experience and common sense. George Herbert in 1641 advised the country parson and his wife to avoid the 'outlandish gums' of the city, and to seek their remedies in the garden and the field: 'For the home-bred medicines are both more easie for the Parson's purse, and more familiar for all men's bodyes.' So 'plantaine, shepherd's purse, knot-grasse' bound up loose bowels and 'Elder, camomill, mallowes, comphrey and smallage made into a Poultis, have done great and rare cures'. There was no fancy about these remedies. Our common weed, *Polygonum aviculare*, was not christened knotgrass for nothing, and its high tannin content combined with the absorbent seeds of plantain would have settled upset stomachs well enough; just as the mucilaginous roots of mallow and comfrey (then more often known as bone-set) made a soothing and effective poultice. So many of our flowers have been named for their medicinal use. Whitlowgrass, feverfew, stitchwort, eyebright, were all named long before the signaturists grafted their 'rational' explanations on to the plants' ancient uses. Perhaps the majority of medicinal herbs did not 'work' in our direct sense, but they were a colourful and pleasingly scented bunch, and could hardly have failed to be some comfort to a sick person. Perhaps this was the reason, as much as convenience of access, why many species were not just gathered in the wild but were taken back to adorn the garden, and still survive there. Mint, woodruff and balm, taken in originally to make 'sweet waters' for sore throats and stomachs, have turned into herbs into our modern culinary sense; tansy, genuinely effective in dispelling worms, was kept on for its pretty yellow button-flowers; honeysuckle first came into gardens to treat asthma, and the shiny green fronds of hart's-tongue fern as an astringent for burns. Gerard anticipated all this, and writing of sweet violets, perhaps the favourite 'wild' garden plant, prefaced his long account of their medicinal virtues with a tribute to their more subtle healing qualities.

> [They] have a great prerogative above others, not onely because the minde conceiveth a certaine pleasure and recreation by smelling and handling of those most odoriferous flours, but also for that very many by these Violets receive ornament and comely grace: for there bee made of them Garlands for the head, Nose-gaies, and poesies, which are delightfull to looke on, and pleasant to smell to, speaking nothing of their appropriate vertues; yea Gardens themselves receive by these the greatest ornament of all, chiefest beautie and most gallant grace; and the recreation of the minde which is taken thereby, cannot be but very good and honest: for they admonish and stir up a man to that which is comely and honest.

As wild plants were brought into gardens for their medicinal value and later simply to delight the eye, so an even greater number of hardy imports from all over the world began to escape and spread out along the waysides. Some of these were pure opportunists and found their own way out; others, too ambitious, too big for their roots, or just plain unfashionable, were given a helping hand with the shovel. And so began those marvellous jostlings of colour at the edges of villages, the exotic and the native side by side, with the foreigner as likely to advance steadfastly along the lanes as the home-grown weed was to nip back into the vegetable patch. They are now a thoroughly established and rightly loved part of our wayside flora and, though many of them are out of fashion in modern gardens, they strike pleasant echoes along the lanes, a reminder that these roads were once routes for strolling and talking between villages as well as short-cuts between motorways.

Some of the most widely established plants came straight from the herb garden – horseradish, soapwort, feverfew, and, in most parts of Britain (it is native only in the south), the stinking hellebore or setterwort, once given for 'the blacke choler and . . . melancholy'. Someone, suffering more from black humour than blacke choler, once planted a setterwort plumb beneath one of our local post-boxes, where it continues to thrive. Other herbal immigrants first came to this country with the Romans, who introduced as many medicinal plants to cope with their dietary indiscretions as foods that caused them. Fennel, ground elder and wormwood were all brought over at this time, and expected to deal, respectively, with wind, gout and intestinal worms.

Many of the most persistent and decorative garden escapes are also from southern Europe – alkanet, honesty, dame's-violet, rose-of-sharon, everlasting-pea, dusty miller, purple toadflax, globe thistle, half a dozen cranesbills, and scores of what the gardening catalogues aptly call 'hardy perennials'. Yet some of the most solidly rooted colonists of the English lanes have come from halfway across the world – goldenrod from North America, japanese knotweed from the Far East. This last plant is so well established in some areas that it is regarded as more of a menace than a curiosity. In one Cornish locality in the 1930s it actually earned the title 'Hancock's curse' – having originally spread from the garden of someone with that name. There is a reliable report that a house in the same area was reduced in price by £100 because its garden was overrun with japweed.

And then there is monbretia from South Africa, botany's own challenge to apartheid. Monbretia, *Crocosmia* × *crocosmiiflora*, is a man-made cross, hybridized from two southern African irises by a French nurseryman. It did not even *exist* – let alone grow wild – until the 1870s. In its 'home' country it is now more common than either of its parents, but is still not known outside gardens. Yet in Britain it is so lively and adaptable that you can see its spikes of warm orange flowers spilling over Cornish cliffs and jostling the heather along Scottish road-

*Garden refugees: hairy bindweed, more
pleasing in its scientific name*
Calystegia pulchra

sides. It deserves a more cheerful and expressive name than the bland dog-Latin label it is stuck with at present. Geoffrey Grigson, arguing that such flowers should 'be naturalised by name no less than by culture', made the admirable suggestion of tiger's teeth ('who cares if there are no tigers in the Cape?').

The curious thing is that, even 6000 miles away from the Cape, tiger's teeth does not look the least bit out of place. Colonizing plants have a knack of mingling and merging, of making themselves at home. It is hard to credit that winter heliotrope, whose heart-shaped winter leaves blanket many waysides as unaffectedly as those of its larger cousin butterbur, did not even arrive in our gardens until 1806. At about the same time the yellow rock stonecrop *Sedum forsteranum* (then *S. rupestre*) was beginning to creep out of rockeries in East Anglia. By 1901, a local botanist noted that it had 'taken possession of a tract of land some miles square in north-east Norfolk'. It is still modestly frequent in hedgebanks about Southrepps. I have seen a formidable thicket of *Rosa rugosa*, from Japan, growing on a sandy heath behind Aldeburgh in Suffolk, only 100 yards from a fen full of Caucasian giant hogweed whose trunks matched some of the willows for size. In western Ireland, South American fuchsia grows so well, so *normally*, that they make hedges from it.

The colonizers will invade almost any habitat. Stationmasters' lupins edge along railway embankments. The delicate purple-tinged daisy *Erigeron mucronatus* (from Mexico, *c.* nineteenth century) has found its way to the venerable walls of Merton College, Oxford (*c.* thirteenth century). In my own parish autumn crocuses have reached the borders of the A41, and a colony of opium poppies has appeared, mysteriously, in a deep excavation in the moated fortifications of our Norman castle. Whether their seed drifted in from the present keeper's herbaceous beds, or were unearthed relics of some ancient physic garden, does not really affect the point: all garden plants have their roots in the wild (*Papaver somniferum*'s were probably in central Europe) and don't need much encouragement to return to it.

Yet of all garden escapes, I cannot think of one which has blended more thoroughly and pleasingly into our natural landscape than the monkey flower, *Mimulus guttatus*. It is an absurdly inappropriate name for a plant whose beautiful yellow flowers are as bright and buxom as nasturtiums, but no one has coined an alternative as yet. Monkey flower came to this country from the damp and foggy Aleutian Islands off Alaska, and seems to have found the similar climes of upland Britain very congenial. It can be found all over the country, but it is along the edges of wide rivers in the Scottish lowlands, by West Country fords and Welsh mill streams and brooks high in the Yorkshire dales that it seems most at home – or perhaps shines out most conspicuously against the dark encircling moors. I shall never forget finding it after a morning's fruitless botanizing on the Cumberland coast one parched day in June 1975. The dunes had been as sterile and burnt as a desert, the cliff pastures grazed bare, and Tony and I had driven back disconsolately over the fells near Eskdale, past drystone walls braided with downy rose and foxglove. It was a particularly vivid shock of foxgloves in some rough pasture that made us stop and peer over the stones. And there, caught in a gap in a farther wall, like a painted glass door, was a sheet of purest liquid yellow. The gap, when we came to it, was a culvert for a brook, and the yellow glare, drifts of monkey flower along its edge, their reflections so brightly glittering on the surface of the water that they seemed to merge with the sharp pebbles beneath. We followed the stream up the hill towards a farmhouse, with gold rippling round our feet. At the head of the gulley cut by the brook was a fen of sorts, and here the monkey flower merged with sedges, water mint and forget me not, and, extraordinarily, with another escaped North American *Mimulus*, wild musk. They had both travelled 4000 miles from their natural homes in little more than a century and a half, yet were tucked as naturally in this secluded valley as if they were as old as the hills themselves.

PART THREE

Field

Our image of fields and their plants is as ambiguous as our image of woods. When the Rev. C. A. Johns called his famous textbook *Flowers of the Field*, he was referring not just to open farmlands, but to the 'open air', the whole of the rural landscape. We even call identification books of this kind 'field guides' – though inside you will find the word used in a more limited sense, and attached to a motley collection of some twenty flowers: a rose that is properly a plant of hedgerow and scrub, four meadow perennials, a dozen annual arable weeds, one tree (a maple) that is found in woods as much as in the open, and not a single grass.

Yet we know that to the farmer the meaning of 'field' has none of this airiness. It is his basic unit of space, the division by which he organizes his work and his cycle of crops. Field systems are quite literally plans drawn on the land. Their outlines are so decisive and persistent that from an aircraft flying at the height of Mount Everest you can still make sense of them on the ground. And you will see not just the current boundaries but traces of earlier enclosures which, centuries later, still influence the crops that grow above them.

At ground level they can be awe-inspiring. If you travel round the ancient clay-lands of west Suffolk, threading between the immense embanked ditches that line the fields, you will see the effort farmers were prepared to make to keep their crops in and the water out. The message of those banks – the stronger now the field oaks and elms that once topped them are vanishing – is quite unequivocal: the forest stops here.

BEATING THE BOUNDS

Fields are above all about *organization*, about selection, deployment, demarcation; and it is this which determines the plants that grow in and around them, as well as much of our attitude towards them. The first fields were little more than clearings in the forest, and it's doubtful if prehistoric farmers bothered to mark their boundaries as assertively as we do today. Yet there is not much doubt that they had the ability to do so had they wished; that they could, within limits, pick and choose the trees they cleared, and maybe leave particularly striking (or just intractable) specimens standing as landmarks.

It was a group of Danish archaeologists who demonstrated just how effective stone axes could be in forest clearance. In 1953 they obtained permission to fell 2 acres of Draved Forest in Jutland. They borrowed flint axe-heads from the National Museum, and had them fitted to ashwood handles modelled on that of the neolithic Sigerslev axe. The experiment went badly at first. Two professional lumberjacks, hired to help with the felling, were unable to shake off the habits acquired over years of working with modern steel axes. Swinging vast blows from the shoulder, they succeeded in breaking several of the 4000-year-old axe-heads. The less athletic – and, as it proved, more adaptable – archaeologists then took over the felling themselves and, developing a technique of short, quick strokes from the elbow, were able to fell trees with trunk diameters of a foot in less than half an hour. Between them, three fellers were able to clear about 150 square yards of forest every hour.

By the middle ages individual trees and bushes were certainly being spared in order to mark out boundaries, and they figure largely in the legal descriptions of these known as 'perambulations'. These are amongst the earliest documents which describe pieces of countryside in recognizable detail. Oliver Rackham quotes a particularly evocative one for Hurstbourne Priors, Hampshire, dated 901 AD:

> Start from Twyford along the road to Bracken Ridge, from there along the road to Carrion Barrow; then in a straight line to the pear tree; then along the road to Ceardic's Barrow; then to Withy Grove; then to the road that shoots over the ditch; then along the road to the pollard oak; from there along the road from where it adjoins the wood . . . by the little hedge along the spinney . . . along the hedge to the old maple tree . . . from there to the hoar [lichen-covered] apple tree; then along the ditch out to the River Test; to its southern bank; then along the bank; then below the timber weir to the northern bank; along the bank back to Twyford.

OVERLEAF: *Musk thistle and fieldscape. Powys*

How many surveyors today, I wonder, could tell the difference between a crab apple and a wild pear? Yet in a survey of perambulations in the *Cartularium Saxonicum*, Oliver Rackham finds trees mentioned as boundary features in more than half of the descriptions. The majority are thorns (still the most common boundary tree), but there are frequent references to species which, like the wild pear, are now much scarcer. How was it that such patently mortal features found their way into what were presumably meant to be relatively permanent legal documents? A barrow or a river is one thing; only the most massive upheavals in the landscape would be likely to disturb it. But a tree, even an oak (one of the most commonly mentioned boundary trees), could vanish overnight from fire or felling. One answer, of course, is that there were very few alternatives. Medieval boundaries passed through a countryside lonelier and less built on than our own, on which trees were often the only landmarks. And though the Anglo-Saxons would have had no illusions about the life-spans of plants, they knew that trees stood a good chance of outliving most of their man-made structures.

Boundary trees do seem to have had a special kind of indemnity, growing as they do at the edges of things, and often seeming ancient enough to be above claims of ownership. Even on the most ruthlessly efficient modern farms they are usually the last trees to be cleared. The relative security of the ground itself along boundary lines must have added to the surveyors' confidence in natural land-marks; if the old thorn died there was a good chance that it would survive in the form of a self-sown successor.

And it seems as if their confidence was justified. There are cases where boundary trees mentioned in Anglo-Saxon charters are still represented today by the same species marking the same point in the boundary. Some of these are the Gospel Oaks which are commemorated in so many place names. These trees marked the point in 'the beating of the bounds' where the gospel for Rogation Day was read. The beating of the bounds, a ceremony which still survives in a few parishes, is a remarkable amalgam of pagan plant ritual, Christian benediction and civic lecture. The processions through the fields are traditionally held around

Ascension Day, but they almost certainly date from pre-Christian times, when fertility rites were performed to encourage the crops. They appeared as a regular Christian ceremony round about the fifth century, principally as a vehicle for the blessing of the fields. Later they also began to serve as a convenient way of confirming the parish boundaries, though this was of secondary importance to their religious function. George Herbert, in *The Country Parson* (1652), defended the custom, and listed its 'manifold advantages', which included, '(1) a blessing of God for the fruits of the field; (2) Justice in the preservation of bounds; (3) Charitie, in living walking and neighbourly accompanying one another, with reconciling of differences at that time, if they be any. . . .'

'Justice in the preservation of bounds' was difficult to uphold when maps were scarce, and an annual perambulation around the boundaries was as good a way as any of refreshing people's memories about where they ran. Nor was it just the bounds themselves that were beaten. Adventurous youngsters were taught literally to know their place, and had the parish limits impressed upon them by painful physical experiences. They were dragged through hedges, pushed up trees, dunked in ponds.

These rather un-Christian aides-memoire have mostly disappeared. But the parades still continue, sanctified equally it seems by Pan and the Church. At Lichfield in Staffordshire, the clergy and choir of the cathedral carry elm boughs on the procession and stop along the route to read the Gospel at eight points where there used to be wells. When the walk is over they return to the cathedral and arrange the elm boughs around the font.

Elms have always figured large in parish mythology. Brooding, clustered, growing to immense heights and great ages, they have been the paramount trees of settlements. As far as we can tell from pollen records they were a popular tree even in neolithic times, and their boughs and foliage were gathered for cattle and probably even human food. Perhaps the tradition of the village 'clump' began as far back as this. Yet 5000 years ago the climate was probably warm enough for our native elms to set fertile seeds; and their patterning in the landscape must have been rather different from today. They would have been more widespread, and the varieties (and possibly hybrids) that exist in our two or three native species would have been closely intermingled. Then the climate deteriorated and the elms no longer ripened their seed, and the majority of trees now spread by suckers. If these have the opportunity to grow into mature trees, they will form what is called a 'clone' – a set of vegetative carbon copies of the parent tree. The size and age of the offspring vary enormously, of course; but in the details of bark texture, branch pattern and leaf shape their origins will be unmistakable. Look at a line of field elms – even dead ones – from a distance and you can pick out the cloning families. Their shape and habit will match up like receding images in a mirror.

The readiness of elms to put out suckers is the chief reason why single villages, and sometimes even single farms, often had uniquely distinctive elm trees. The raw material out of which these settlements wrought one of the more far-reaching, unwitting acts of landscape gardening in our history was something of a genetic lucky dip: perhaps three main species – wych in the north, English in the south, smooth-leaved in the east – and any number of varieties in between. Beyond that were the subtler differences between individual trees, which gave clones their identity. A landowner who was after a covert by his house or in the corner of a field needed to do no more than let a parent elm sucker freely. If he wanted a hedge, he would cut out the suckers and plant them in lines along the field edge.

Round the village of Knapwell in Cambridgeshire the outlines of a much larger medieval settlement are still marked by lines of vast pollard elms that are almost certainly of common parentage. The modern village is not much more than a single row of houses, yet for hundreds of yards on either side of the street these ancient trees plot the routes of the vanished lanes and closes and old estate boundaries. Here and there they have been enveloped by the new village, marooned by bungalows, and they rise up in the gaps as indifferent and incongruous as standing stones. One props up a garden shed. Another has fallen

Floral borders – field mouse-ear by the edge of the old Foss Way. Gloucestershire, May

over in a farm pond, yet is still sprouting new branches up towards the light.

The trees are so gnarled and distorted by centuries of pollarding that it is difficult to date them accurately. But the oldest may date back as far as the late medieval period. The villagers call them the Dodds, no doubt from 'dodderel', which is a common local word for a pollard in eastern England. (Interestingly, 'dodman' is also an East Anglian dialect word for snail and, looking at the trunks hunched out in the field, reduced to round and hollow shells for the most part, it is easy to imagine the words having a common root.)

Yet a few are still alive, protected by Tree Preservation Orders and their own natural defence mechanisms. Most trees past their prime go into a kind of siege economy known as 'retrenchment', in which they progressively cut down on the number of branches they have to grow and support. Pollarding achieves the same end artificially, which is part of the reason pollard trees live so long. The Knapwell elms have benefited in both ways, and the oldest trees carry no more than a stubble of wispy branches on top of their boles. It's not the most becoming twiggery, but it does give the trees a small measure of protection against Dutch elm fungus, which tends to attack more mature wood. Nevertheless, some have started to succumb, and in the next few years there is a real possibility that Knapwell may lose altogether these extraordinary living memorials that have mapped out its past for four or five centuries.

The passing of these settlement trees is perhaps the greatest tragedy in the saga of elm disease. The wider landscape can, to a certain extent, be restocked. But it is not so easy to make up for the loss of personal, particular trees, which have been part of a community's furniture and have been sat under, walked past and built around for twenty generations.*

---

* Dutch elm disease has now claimed the vast majority of mature elms in Britain. But the disease is now abating, and many surviving root-systems are putting out fresh suckers. It may be some while before we see mature elms in the landscape again, but at least we now have a new feature: the elm bush.

In my own parish one of the richest and oldest rows of trees follows the route of not one boundary but three. I don't think it is a coincidence that in it there is a tree so scarce and striking that even an Anglo-Saxon surveyor might have been impressed. It is a black poplar, nearly 200 years old, and there is not another like it for 10 miles.

I guess I must have glanced at its busy swarm of leaves every spring for half my life. It grows by the course of a stream which has vanished underground and, before I knew much about trees, I took it for some kind of willow. At the time I did not know there was such a thing as an indigenous black poplar, a rugged and shapely tree quite unlike the rather dull 'Italian black' hybrids that are planted along so many suburban highways. Nor, it seemed, did many botanists, if one was to judge by the paucity of records for the native *Populus nigra* var. *betulifolia*. Yet it seems to have been a comparatively frequent tree in medieval times. Even in the nineteenth century it was still plentiful enough to figure in the background of many of Constable's Stour Valley landscapes. Since then the increasing intensity of grassland and riverside management has reduced its numbers so drastically that by the early 1970s there were thought to be less than a thousand mature trees left in Britain, and not a single site where a male and female were close enough for successful pollination. It looked as if the black poplar might achieve the dubious distinction of being the first of our native trees to become extinct in historical times.

To try and establish a more accurate picture of the tree's fortunes, the distinguished East Anglian botanist Edgar Milne-Redhead began a nationwide survey. Once the idea got around that there *were* native, and often unplanted, black poplars about, and their characteristic features became better known, it became clear that there were many more specimens scattered around Britain than had previously been believed. They were discovered in areas as unexpected as the valleys of North Wales and the coastal flats of Lincolnshire. A fine group of maiden

OVERLEAF: *Native black poplar,* Populus nigra *var.* betulifolia. *Constable country, October*

99

trees with barks dark enough, for once, to justify the tree's name, turned up in a sandy meadow by the side of the River Lark at Icklingham in west Suffolk, although they proved to have declined along the Stour and other rivers in the south of the county. By way of compensation, colonies were discovered in previously un-noticed sites in many river valleys in Gloucestershire. The most queerly placed specimen I found myself was in the yard of a demolition company in a wasteland of rubbish-tips and gravel-pits near Heathrow Airport.

The most famous black poplar in the country is probably the Flag Tree at Aston On Clun in Shropshire. This ancient tree stands at the junction of five roads in the heart of the village, and is the centrepiece of the local Arbor Day ceremony. Once a year, on 29 May, the tree is dressed with multicoloured flags and bunting, which are left on until next Arbor Day and then renewed. There are many theories about the origins of the ceremony. Some say it commemorates the marriage of the squire, John Marston, in May 1786, others the birth of his heir. But the date of the ceremony suggests that these associations may have become attached to an already existing celebration. 29 May is also Oak Apple Day – the date of Charles II's birthday and the day he chose for his triumphal entry into London after the Restoration of 1660. Charles declared Oak Apple Day as part of his move to revive the customs discredited by the Puritans, and ordered it to be set aside as a public holiday 'for the dressing of trees'. (It is still celebrated, here and there, by the decking of houses with oak boughs.) But this takes us back further still, to the ancient customs in which the decoration of trees was enacted as a spring fertility ritual – and this may mean that the date of John Marston's marriage was deliberately arranged to coincide with this potent festival.

But why a black poplar – a species with no special magical association – should have got mixed up with fertility rites on a day belonging to the oak is something of a mystery. It is scarcely conceivable that a poplar could live for 300 years, and so the existing tree cannot be the same individual that was first dressed in 1660. Perhaps it was a replacement – convenient and quick-growing – for an oak that had grown on the site previously. But there is no reason, really, why black poplars should not always have been Aston's 'village tree'. Their remarkably gracious and distinctive shape makes them ideal for such a role, and they are frequent enough (it now turns out) in the Welsh border country. One grows on the green in Blakemere, Herefordshire, another outside Eastnor church, 5 miles west of the extraordinary colony of eighty trees on Castlemorton Common, which are still pollarded for use in the village by the Malvern Hills Conservators.

But the most heartening outcome of the search was that there was, after all, a 'married couple' in existence. A farmer's wife in Cheshire had seen a newspaper article about the plight of the poplar, and reported that there were two female trees and one male growing round a neighbour's pond. The female seed proved to have been successfully pollinated, and many seedlings have already been grown from it.

By the spring of 1976 I had become accustomed to the tree's unique profile myself, and that April I recognized – noticed, to tell the truth – my valley poplar for the first time. It was visible half a mile away, tilted over towards the south, its switches of twigs ablaze with crimson catkins. Closer to I could make out all the typical features of *P. nigra*: the gnarled and furrowed bark, covered with huge round burrs; the sweep of the main branches downwards, close to the ground; and the *upwards* sweep of the bunches of shoots. Even the lean was in character, and has been getting black poplars a bad name as far back as the middle ages. In an Essex court roll for 1422 there is a reference to 'one ancient and decayed [black] poplar growing out too far over the King's highway'. But the farmer on whose land my tree was growing gave a new slant on this specimen's spectacular tilt. Apparently there had been two poplars at one time, very close to one another, and they had grown apart into a V, each searching for light and space. The elder of the two trees had been felled only a few years ago, as it was nearing the end of its life.

It was remarkable that two black poplars should have survived so long in what is predominantly arable countryside. They are trees of open, damp meadowland,

OVERLEAF: *The ancient pollard boundary elms in the deserted medieval village of Knapwell, Cambridgeshire*

and are very vulnerable to ploughing and drainage. Since they rarely produce suckers, the felling of a mature tree usually means its extinction on that spot. And since the timber is now regarded as worthless (though it was used for crucks in medieval buildings) black poplars are rarely replanted. Yet here on this ancient boundary line, between two farms, two parishes, two counties, the surviving tree has escaped even being cut back. Just what its future prospects are, I would not like to say. When I measured its girth, it was nearly 15 feet, making the tree somewhere between 150 and 200 years old. This is a good span for a poplar, and already the first signs of old age – the shedding of the arched lower branches – has begun.* Yet when it does die, it may not mean the end of black poplars in this valley. Whilst I was searching through the hedge on the far side of the trunk I found what I thought was a drooping branch from the main tree. But it turned out to be a quite separate shoot, sprung, as far as I could tell, from the now invisible stump of the felled tree, like a shoot from a coppice stool. It was already 4 feet high and in the shelter of the hedge stood a good chance of surviving.

Left to straggle together, or deliberately trimmed and trained so that their branches start to intermesh, a row of boundary trees forms the beginnings of a hedge. And a more precise definition of a hedge than that it is difficult to give. The word goes back to the Anglo-Saxon, and in our own time has become so all-embracing that we use it as one of our basic terms of enclosing. Hedges can be tall or stubby, woody or bushy, dense or 'gappy', ditched, banked or propped up with fencing, but seen in the context of a pattern of fields and paths, they are all quite clearly boundaries, devices whose function is to limit and protect. Although we have become accustomed to their destruction, it is difficult to imagine the English countryside without hedges. They give it order and continuity, as if they were the signature to a contract between humans and the land. They are kept in check, but

---

* The top of the poplar blew off in 1983 and it nows grows like a naturally pruned pollard.

assert their independence and liveliness every spring, not only with their own greenery, but with the primroses and cow parsley that flourish along their supporting banks. Yet until quite recently the accepted view of hedges was that they were all legacies of the parliamentary enclosures, man-made fences that were rarely more than 200 years old and certainly not worth the sentimental affection lavished upon them.

Now, thanks largely to the work of Dr Max Hooper, we know that many of our hedges are vastly older than this; and that they are indeed the kind of subtle alloy of human and natural activity that they appear in the field. The earliest known reference to a British hedge is to one erected by Ida of Northumbria round Bamburgh in 547 AD. Throughout the medieval period hedges figure in court rolls and perambulations, and one estimate suggests that as much as half the hedged and walled landscape of England dates from between the Bronze Age and the seventeenth century. Many of these ancient hedges still exist, and flourish in precisely the same sites in which they were first described maybe 1000 years ago.

It was while Max Hooper was investigating hedges whose date of origin was known from written records that he began to notice the correlation between the age of a hedge and the variety of species of tree and shrub growing in it. Many hundreds of hedges later the now well-known equation emerged: the age of a hedge in centuries equals the average number of shrub species in a 30-yard stretch. It seems an incongruously tidy rule for what is, after all, a collection of living plants; and it is only a statistical approximation, a rule of thumb. But it works quite well on the majority of hedges in England, which raises the question of just *how* new species join a hedge so regularly over the centuries.

By coincidence, the line of trees in which the black poplar stands is itself an old hedge. It's not managed any more and cattle have eaten away much of the lower foliage, so that its structure stands out like a cut-away diagram. It is very rich in species, containing fourteen (including aspen, spindle and two species of willow) in not much more than 200 yards. The way they are growing suggests that what is now a loose cordon of trees strung together by barbed wire was once a conventional stockproof hedge. When a hedge is cut and laid, the trunks and vertically growing branches are partially sliced through close to the ground, and then bent over until they are almost horizontal. In derelict hedges this produces a distinctive pattern of growth in which trees carry substantial branches close to, and parallel to, the ground. This pattern is characteristic of a number of sections of this line of trees, and is particularly easy to see because of the way the cattle keep the trunks and low branches clear of new shoots. They also browse away most of the seedling trees which spring up on the ground beneath. In a working hedge these seedlings stand a rather better chance of surviving because of the protective bushiness around them, and some are able to spread into the gaps opened up by damage or disease. Most will have originated with fruit fallen from shrubs already in the hedge, but a few will be of new species, whose seed has blown in or been carried in by birds. A kind of succession takes place, with regular hedge-cutting helping to give new arrivals a chance against the expansive, established shrubs. And the rate is seemingly very constant: one species per century per 30 yard stretch.

Not a quarter of a mile from the black poplar there are some old hedges that demonstrate the strengths and weaknesses of the formula. They line an ancient track that runs along the crest of the hills for more than 5 miles, and which may be a neolithic ridgeway. It was certainly well-established by the fourteenth century, and by the time of the first written reference in 1357 already had a name – Shokersweye, possibly meaning 'robbers' road'. (This was softened to Sugarsway in the eighteenth century, and is preserved today in the names of two roads which overlie either end of the track – Shootersway and Sugar Lane.) It would be presuming a lot to assume that the boundary hedges are necessarily the same age; but the species count does suggest that they are as much as 800 years old. This is a great age, and during its gradual evolution a hedge becomes a kind of living fossil, preserving in its pattern of growth evidence of the changes that have happened to it in the past. Reading back this evidence is, if anything, more fascinating than simple hedge-dating. Some of it has to do with deliberate plantings in the hedge

Foxgloves, lovers of acid soils. Eskdale, Cumbria, July

that upset the formula: orchard trees set down near farm gates; gaps made good with rows of beech, perhaps in the nineteenth-century heyday of beech planting; and along the metalled section now known as Shootersway, simpler two and three species hedges that in their regularity and straightness exactly express the era when the track was modernized. Yet there is one 40 yard section of these enclosure hedges where the old pattern reasserts itself in an abrupt and graphic jump. Just here a great ash lies back from the road, preserved by the developers, I imagine, either because it defeated their axes or touched their hearts. The clipped and symmetrical quickset hedges approach it on either side, fray at the edges and then dip back towards the ash in a riotous crescent of oak and hazel and wild rose.

I have known these hedges for not much more than a quarter of a century. Yet even in that comparatively short time it has been possible to watch the processes of succession at work. For a few years the hedges were allowed to grow so profusely that it became difficult to walk between them, and partridges nested in the path. More recently many sections have been cut to ground level, or burned away completely by stubble fires. Yet, the following spring, new shoots have always appeared from the ramified root systems in the banks. You can still count eight species to a stretch even when the shrubs are only 6 inches tall. It is in these temporary gaps that what may turn out to be this century's contribution to the species tally – the sycamore – has sown itself from nearby copses.

There is, I confess, much room for speculation in the analysis of hedges, and nowhere more than in attempts to establish their origins. Were the Shokersweye hedges, for instance, once simple rows of thorn or hazel, planted out by a twelfth-century farmer? (They used to wrap nuts and berries in hanks of twine and set them in shallow trenches.) Or do they represent surviving strips of primeval woodland, left as boundaries when the fields were first cleared? This was another common way of starting hedges in the medieval period.

One clue is that there is a good deal of bluebell and dog's mercury growing under the hedges. These, as we have seen, are predominantly woodland plants, and they will only colonize new hedges very slowly. Their presence in quantities along a hedgebank is a good sign that trees have never been absent from the site. (Though it is all too easy to be deceived about the date when this presumed woodland clearance occurred. Not long ago I went searching for a primrose copse I had not visited since I was a child. I could find no trace of the wood, and wondered if, all these years later, I was confused about the site. But I did find what looked like an elegant example of a relict medieval wood-edge, complete with a dozen species of tree and shrub, and bluebell, dog's mercury and primrose growing along its whole length. Then I realized it was all that was left of my copse. The trees had been cleared the previous year to make an arable field, and out amidst the spring corn the last obstinate bluebells were pushing up their shoots.)

The primrose, a flower which perhaps above all others we expect to see on old hedgebanks, is the one conspicuously missing from Shokersweye. It grows in woods close by, and its absence is the one piece of evidence which suggests the hedges may *not* be woodland relics. Yet, equally, it may be that this flinty and chalky hilltop site is too dry for them. In 1944 Professor R. Good made an extensive study in Dorset of the distribution of primroses in relation to factors like rainfall and soil-type. He travelled 'every road and major track in Dorset, many of them more than once', and discovered a distinct pattern as to where primroses did, and did not, grow. In the west of the county they occurred equally in woods and hedgebanks. In the east they were largely confined to woods. Nowhere did they grow in hedgebanks but *not* in adjacent woods, and there were two conspicuous areas – one in the extreme east, and one running diagonally north-east across the centre – in which there were virtually no primroses at all.

Professor Good explained this curious pattern in terms of the distribution of soils and rainfall in the county. Primroses prefer damp conditions, and in Dorset the rainfall is noticeably higher in the west than the east. Although hedgebanks dry out more quickly than woods, in the west they are always moist enough to support primroses. In the east only woods on the clays and loams are usually sufficiently humid. The two 'primrose gaps' correspond roughly with chalky or sandy soils, which have a poor water-holding capacity and are the remotest in their micro-climate from the conditions in woodland.

This sounds a convincing and comprehensive explanation, which ought to be applicable to primroses everywhere. The problems come when you consider an area like central Suffolk, where the rainfall is on average 30 inches less than that in east Dorset, but where primroses still grow abundantly in many hedgebanks. The additional factor in the equation may indeed be the history of woodland – the primrose's aboriginal home – on the site.* In west Dorset, for instance, banked hedges may be relics of medieval forest clearance (as they certainly are in parts of central Suffolk) whereas the hedges and roads in the east of the county are probably much later additions to a landscape of open fields and commons. But then the narrow and sinuous contours of medieval banked lanes provide more damp niches than an open-plan landscape. . . .

You are less likely to find simple answers when you start disentangling the history of hedges than ever more convincing evidence of the complex relation-ships between humans and nature which created the medieval landscape.

FIELD WEEDS

Poppies and corn are inseparable. Monet and Van Gogh painted them together. The Romans depicted their crop goddess Ceres with a lighted torch in one hand and a bunch of corn and poppies in the other. We still name the flower after the crop, and see the scarlet of the corn poppies and the dusty yellow of the wheat as the most perfectly elemental colours of high summer.

I can remember the last time I saw a field like that in my own parish. It was August 1959, the summer I left school. I had worked on the harvest that year, stooking behind a reaper and binder, and the poppies had brightened every

---

* It now seems as if the mineral content of the soil may also be important. Primroses appear to favour richer, loamier soils.

112

Primroses, which prefer damper clays.
South-west Dorset, April

moment, caught up like confetti in the sheaves, and blooming on in rows amongst the stubble. For the next few summers I was not to see so much of my home countryside and by the time I was back the poppies had vanished and stooks were part of a memory of an older England. In the space of three or four years the agricultural practices that had supported poppies for so long were swept away. The fields were sown with dressed seed, sprayed with weedkiller, cut by combine, and burned off after harvest. A few poppies survived along the rougher margins and on nearby roadsides, but seemed the duller for growing without that parched yellow backcloth with which they had blended so harmoniously. It was the same across much of Britain, and it looked as if, here at least, an end had come to an association that had lasted nearly 5000 years.

Poppies have grown amongst the corn for so long that no one is sure of their native home. They are flowers which belong not so much to a place as to a way of life, and they have dogged the heels of arable farmers ever since the beginnings of agriculture in the Middle East. Their seeds have been found mixed up with grains of barley in the remains of the Kahun Twelfth Dynasty in Egypt, which prospered before 2500 BC . The Assyrians called them 'the daughters of the field'.

Poppies probably reached this country mixed up with the grain crops of the earliest neolithic settlers, and even on our productive soil they were regarded as signs of life and of the fertility of the earth. British farmers rated the poppy a fairly insignificant weed by the side of docks and thistles, and many common local names – thundercup, thunderflower, lightnings – reflect the ancient belief that poppies must not be picked for fear of a storm, and conversely, perhaps, that whilst they were unpicked the wheat was safe from summer storms. But none of these superstitions can match the magical significance which poppies have acquired in our own supposedly rational century. Every autumn we wear red paper images of the real poppies that, in the summer of 1918, had seemingly sprung miraculously from the blood spilt in the slaughter on Flanders Fields. The ancient symbol of both new life and the harvest, the cutting down, had acquired a terrible new meaning.

But it does not belittle our annual tribute to acknowledge that the great flowering had more to do with dust than with flesh. Like all weeds poppies are dependent on the breaking open of the soil. Battlefields, ploughed fields, bombed sites, building sites – they all mean light and life to a poppy. It was only the introduction of potent new chemical weapons – this time aimed against *them* – that finally drove poppies out of the fields into less troubled habitats.

But, as it turned out, the setback they suffered at the hands of modern agricultural chemicals was only a temporary one. In the early 1970s they began to appear again along waysides and in some of the smaller arable fields. They were not as grandly massed as I remembered them in the 1950s, and seemed to be growing amongst corn that was similarly patchy. Yet here and there in the backlands of East Anglia, and in parts of the West Country where arable farming had never been particularly intensive, you could see again what could be truthfully described as a poppy field. On roadsides and waste patches the red flowers began to be as common and conspicuous as daisies. and, for one glorious summer, the south-facing embankment of the new Bury St Edmunds bypass blazed with scarlet blooms for a solid half-mile where the road had been cut through abandoned farmland.

It was not too difficult to find a reason for this comeback. It occurred during a period of mounting unrest in the Middle East, when the rising costs of oil-based weedkillers caused an increasing number of small farmers to give up spraying their marginal fields. As for the local authorities responsible for roadside verges, many gave up weedkillers altogether, and some even went as far as to abandon mechanized cutting. Poppies have been exploiting weaknesses like this in our defences for thousands of years. 17,000 seeds are produced by every plant – hundreds of millions to a field – and maybe a sixth of these are capable of lying dormant under the soil for at least forty years. No one has yet found a collection of poppy seeds so old that none of them will germinate.

Our feelings towards field poppies are a curious muddle. We love them for their brilliant uncompromising colour and for their associations, if not with medieval magic, at least with childhood summers. Yet they are one of those plants we prefer to see on someone else's land. I don't think this has much to do with their prolific weediness, with the fact that, communally, they can outsmart a farmer simply by outliving him. I think they have become irrevocably fixed in our minds 'inside' the corn. Their simple, floppy petals are seen best as blotches of colour at a distance, away in a field, caught – as they are by their history – a little apart from us, gazed at over a gate, pictured, composed, their romance preserved.

Yet poppies have been the source of intimate garden pleasures, too, and some of their colour variants have been taken into cultivation. The best known cultivars are probably Shirley poppies, with their distinctive white or yellow centres instead of the usual black. The name commemorates the south London village of Shirley, where a Victorian vicar, William Wilks, first noticed the wild ancestors of these poppies growing in a corner of his garden. Shirley was a small village then, and poppies frequently invaded the vicarage garden from the cornfields nearby. But amongst them in the August of 1880 was one solitary flower whose petals had a narrow edge of white. The Rev. Wilks saved the seeds and, out of the 200 plants he raised from them next year, four or five had white-edged petals. He continued selectively breeding them for many years, and eventually succeeded in infusing so much white into the stock that the seeds of his final strain produced flowers which varied in colour from scarlet to pure white, with all shades of pink and all varieties of patched and edged flowers in between – and with the characteristic white or yellow colouring to the centres. The continuing popularity of his poppies is the best memorial to this enterprising vicar; but there is also a pub named the Shirley Poppy by the A232 on the outskirts of Croydon, by which the village has now been swallowed up.

Shirley poppies remind you of the saying that a weed is just a flower growing in the wrong place. In rape fields on the Cotswold limestone I have found field pansies growing with one or two purple 'ears', and a few with perfectly balanced dark cheek patches, which exactly recall the face pattern of large garden pansies. Perhaps the little heartsease played some part in their evolution. But by and large it

Common, field or corn poppy.
Norfolk, July

is odd how rarely field weeds have been 'improved' for the garden. You would have thought their record of hardiness and long flowering would have endeared them to nurserymen on the search for new winter delights. Many of the most attractive – and I am thinking particularly of the speedwells and dead-nettles – are almost permanently in flower. In the very mild winter of 1974/5 I was able to find more than thirty of these opportunist weeds in full bloom; and so well adapted did they seem that it was impossible to say whether they were the last flowers of the old year or the first of the new.

Even on looks alone, there are cornfield weeds that would warrant a place in a garden of miniatures. I cannot think of any of the grander British wild flowers which can match the delicacy of venus's looking-glass, which carries at the end of its long seed capsules tiny, purple star-flowers, caught like cogs amongst the spokes of the calyx. They have something of the colour and elegance of dwarf gentians, yet you can easily miss the plant in the chalky fields it haunts. It is rarely more than 6 inches high, with thin, oddly crimped leaves that seem to weave between the corn stalks. It closes its flowers in dull weather. And the most astonishing part of the plant – the source of that curious name – lies hidden inside the seed capsule: a cluster of shining oval fruits, like brilliantly polished brass mirrors.

Perhaps all that has kept these weeds out of the nurserymen's catalogues is a collective bad name, the shadow cast by centuries of attack by 'good husbandmen'. The first full list of troublesome arable weeds was published by John Fitzherbert in the *Boke of Husbandry*, in 1523. He wrote, 'In the later ende of May is tyme to wede thy corne. There be divers manner of wedes as Thistles, Kedlockes [charlock], Dockes, Cockle, Darnolde [darnel], Gouldes [corn marigold], and Dog fennell [stinking mayweed].' 300 years later William Pitt drew up a similar list in his *General View of the Agriculture of the County of Leicestershire* (1809). Rather less of a nuisance, apparently, were hemp-nettle, white dead-nettle, field bindweed, shepherd's needle, corn scabious, cornflower, coltsfoot, dog daisy, groundsel, scorpion grass, silverweed, corn mint, tares, goosegrass, nettles, poppies.

It is a familiar company, and there can't be many fields which don't still carry a few of these species. Yet it is not so much the continuity (to be expected) which is remarkable, as the changes. 150 years of agricultural improvements, of drills and seed screens and herbicides, have drastically reduced the populations of most of our field weeds. Ironically, it is the most colourful that seem to have suffered the worst. Cornflowers and corncockle (a deep purple campion, if you have never been lucky enough to see one) are all but extinct in Britain. Corn marigolds are now scarce even in the sandy soils they once used to blanket.

Weeds, by definition, are plants that take advantage of human activity, and their fortunes are inevitably linked with changes in agriculture. New crops bring new weeds. Yet the slightest lapse in a farmer's vigilance may bring back infestations of the old, in such brilliant, explosive masses after their long dormancies that, to most onlookers, they do not seem to be weeds at all; and the folk memory of what a field of flowers must once have looked like is kept alive a little longer.

As we have already seen, many of our arable weeds migrated here from southern Europe with the successive waves of early settlers. Remains of corn poppy, fat hen and red dead-nettle first crop up in deposits of the Beaker people, who came here from Spain in the Bronze Age. Corn marigold, scarlet pimpernel and corncockle begin to appear in Roman layers. The southerly origins of many of these plants is highlighted by their response to our capricious climate. They are conspicuously more common after a run of hot summers has enabled them to ripen their seed; and the most sensitive of them, conversely, depleted after a succession of wet, cool summers.

Yet they could scarcely get off the ground as weeds if they weren't adaptable to climate, and a much greater influence on how they fare is the way the land is farmed. The first organized attack upon arable weeds was the introduction of the seed-drill by Jethro Tull in the mid-eighteenth century. By sowing crops in straight rows it opened up the possibility of regular hoeing. This reduced the overall population of weeds, but probably affected all species in much the same way. It was not until mechanized threshers began to replace hand winnowing, and it became possible to sift crop seeds from weed seeds because of their different sizes, that some species began to decline sharply.

Up till that moment even the best-hoed arable fields must have looked occasionally like commemorative flower-beds. Only half a century ago, Edward Salisbury was able to write about 'a cornfield near Oxford in 1926, the year when the Prince of Wales was President of the British Association meeting there, which looked as if it had been sown for the occasion, since it was red, white and blue with Poppies, Mayweed, and *Centaurea cyanus*.' *Centaurea cyanus* is the cornflower or bluebottle, one of the best-loved field weeds, but also one of the most damaging. Even John Clare, who rarely had a bad word to say of any flower, wrote of 'blue cornbottles . . . troubling the cornfields with their destroying beauty'. Another striking blue weed was the corn larkspur, *Delphinium ambiguum*. J. S. Henslow, who was Professor of Botany at Cambridge over 150 years ago, refers to the hills at Quy near Cambridge being quite blue with its flowers.

As for the reds, the chief rival to the field poppy was pheasant's eye, *Adonis annua*. This is a small scarlet buttercup originally from the Mediterranean, so attractive and so abundant once that its flowers used to be sold in Covent Garden Market under the name 'Red Morocco'. Early in the nineteenth century it was even plentiful in the cornfields round Acton W4, which was then still a village.

And what can *purple* flowers have looked like amongst the wheat? Purple horned poppy, *Roemeria hybrida*, was once frequent in the chalky fields of East Anglia. The extraordinary field cow-wheat, *Melampyrum arvense*, with its flamboyant stacks of purple and yellow bracts (likened by Geoffrey Grigson to the storeys of a pagoda) grew abundantly in the Isle of Wight, above the Undercliff between Ventnor and St Lawrence. The first record on the island was in 1823:

> A few years later Dr Bromfield, who found it in vast abundance in its present locality, carefully investigated its history. Local tradition asserted that the plant was imported with wheat-seed from 'foreign parts' – some said Spain, some

Old weed: corn marigold in barley, Nairnshire, July. 'Gold' was once such an abundant weed that several Anglo-Saxon villages were named from it

Jersey, others, with more probability, from Norfolk. He learnt that it was the custom at harvest time to pull up the weed with the greatest care, and carry it off the fields in bags, and to burn it, picking up the very seeds from the ground wherever they could be perceived lying. The bread, he was told, made from the wheat on the farms above the Undercliff was not so dark coloured and 'hot' as it used to be, and that the 'droll' plant was less plentiful than formerly. Its local name was 'Poverty Weed', with reference, no doubt, not only to the way in which it impoverished the soil, but also to the fact that the seeds, becoming mixed with the corn, rendered the latter of small value in the market.

Flowers of the Field, JOHN VAUGHAN, 1906

These days poverty weed is confined to a single bank above the Ventnor Undercliff, and a few scattered locations in Wiltshire and East Anglia. Cornflowers and corn delphiniums are more likely to be found on rubbish tips than in wheatfields. Poppies, as we have seen, have temporarily returned, but will likely be driven out again.

Those of us who do not have to make our living growing food may regret this, but the preservation of those sheets of colour beneath the corn is one concession we cannot in all conscience ask farmers to make. So, for the present at least, we must make do with the more modest displays that appear on sites like roadside verges, which arable weeds have colonized from nearby fields and on which they live in precarious exile amongst the native perennials.

Yet it has to be said that the modern policy of saturating fields with herbicide may, in the long run, prove to be no more in the farmer's interest than it is in the botanist's. There is evidence that some of the faster-multiplying weeds, like chickweeds and speedwells, are evolving strains resistant to current weedkillers; and, released from competition from the more sensitive weeds, are actually increasing where there is regular spraying. Coarse wild grasses (which are normally immune to weedkillers developed for spraying on grass and cereal crops) also benefit from the reduced competition. Indeed, the end product of all the processes of cultivation, from sowing to harvesting, is the selection and encouragement of weeds which approximate closer and closer to the height, fruiting period, seed size and pesticide resistance of the crop species. This is precisely what is happening in some arable areas of the Near East, where weed seeds are becoming increasingly difficult to separate out. In the end the more varied but more easily differentiated weed flora of less heavily managed fields may prove to be preferable.

In the meantime new crops will bring with them, as impurities, new weeds. Since the Second World War, for instance, the increasing quantities of seed imported from America has led to a whole range of newcomers, and to increases in the populations of what were previously just casuals, including green nightshade (*Solanum sarrachoides*), one of the prairie tumbleweeds (*Salsola pestifer*) in carrot fields, and tarweeds or fiddlenecks (*Amsinckia* spp.) amongst grain crops. I have seen sandy fields in Suffolk completely bordered with the orange and yellow flowers of these Californian forget-me-nots.

One new crop (an edible variety of the normally poisonous lupin) has been through the entire gamut of roles that it is possible for a plant to play, beginning as a wild flower, then taken into gardens, escaping again as a naturalized 'weed' and now being deliberately grown as a source of vegetable protein. It will be as fascinating to see how a field of lupins appears to us through this welter of associations as it will be to see which weeds turn out to be its close companions.

GRASSLANDS

In the preface to one of his later collections, the nineteenth-century Northamptonshire poet John Clare records that it was 'a very old custom among villagers in summertime to stick a piece of greensward full of field flowers and place it as an ornament in their cottages which ornaments are called Midsummer Cushions'. Knowing what pieces of greensward must have looked like before the advent of chemical sprays, it is hard to believe they needed any extra decoration to turn them into ornaments. What flowers, I wonder, did the villagers stick in? More of those that bloomed there anyway, or some of those that did not? Did they add favourites from their cottage gardens, and, like modern flower arrangers, twigs and mosses for sculptural effect?

Almost anything would have looked well placed. Despite the terrible attrition our flowery grassland has suffered since the Second World War, we all have a Midsummer Cushion somewhere in our memories – a clearing in a wood, a downland bank, the corner of a meadow. A piece of greensward still seems the most perfect, the most thoroughly *natural* setting for wild flowers. Yet, to tell the truth, there is scarcely such a thing as 'natural' grassland in Britain. There are patches of naturally treeless ground, growing grass, on cliff-tops and river banks, for example; but the great sweeps of open ground that we normally understand by the term grassland are, in one important sense, artificial. They were cleared of forest by humans and have been kept clear by grazing animals. The constant nibbling back of new growth not only holds up the establishment of new trees but encourages the spread of plants that have the ability to extend themselves horizontally, and the grasses are especially well equipped in this respect. But grazing traditionally had one other botanically important effect. By keeping the ground free of shade it also provided an opportunity for plants from a variety of open habitats to come together.

You can see this very strikingly on chalk downland. Walk across a 100-yard stretch from beechwood edge to bare chalk, say, and you will see clustered together species whose natural habitats are as diverse as woodland clearings and mountain crags. Start in the scrub, which is the true intermediate stage between grassland and wood. If you have any lingering feelings that this is not really a plant community at all but some kind of woody refuse, look at it first in autumn. Chalk scrub often has as many as twenty different species of young trees and shrubs, and they are more distinctive in their autumn tints than at any other time: the bronzed golds of beech, the lemon of blackthorn, the reds and oranges of field maple; claret dogwood, scarlet guelder rose; the feathery white plumes of old man's beard, the black berries of buckthorn and privet, and the extraordinary shocking-

New weed: rosebay willowherb spreading from railway line in Aberdeenshire. Rosebay was a scarce plant in Britain until frequent upheavals of the land this century gave it an opportunity to expand its range

pink fruits of spindle. Then go back in the springtime and crawl through the scrub on your hands and knees. You will not see many plants in flower in the deep shade, but if you find just one fly orchid you may feel that all the discomfort has been worthwhile. The dusky inflorescences, velvet-bodied, blue-waisted, swim up in front of your face in the gloom, scarcely credible as flowers. Move your head a foot to one side and they may vanish from sight, and you begin to find that you are stalking them, not even like vegetable insects, but like flesh-and-blood animals. I have more than once caught myself looking uneasily over my shoulder when I have been hunting fly orchids in dense scrub. In open limestone grassland in the north they seem, by contrast, contrived and stiff, as if the flies had been impaled.

Out of the scrub and into the grassland proper, the first plants you will find are the tall species whose ancestral habitat is woodland clearings – marjoram, scabious, valerian, and bush and tufted vetches. Then, on the grazed turf, the squatter herbs begin: rock-rose, wild thyme and harebell, which you will also see far above the tree-level on mountain rocks; milkwort, from cliff-tops and heaths; and many species which are associated with stable sand dunes, for instance centaury and its greyish-leaved cousin yellow-wort, kidney vetch, bee orchid, and restharrow, whose leaves have a scent curiously reminiscent of vaseline.

Ant-hills, which can be common on old grassland, have their own special communities. The fine, well-drained soil favours species which are able to form compact, moisture-conserving tufts or rosettes – salad burnet, thyme and rock-rose again, and the lemon-flowered mouse-ear hawkweed. They also seem particularly attractive to various members of the bedstraw family, and I have seen three different species, squinancywort, field madder and lady's bedstraw, on a single mound. My fantasy is to find five, with the rare slender bedstraw, *Galium pumilum*, in the chalky soil at the base, and its chalk-hating look-alike, *Galium saxatile*, in the more acid soil on the crown.

It is the distribution of the plants in the shortest turf that poses the most fascinating questions. The frog orchid you would expect; in the north it is not uncommon on mountain grassland. But where did the stemless thistle hide out before the spread of pastured grasslands? I have never seen it away from the most closely grazed turf on the southern chalk, its rosettes of prickly leaves lying flush with the grass, flat and inconspicuous – until you sit down on them. Its habit of lurking in the most temptingly soft grass of beauty spots has earned it the nickname of picnic thistle.

Some grassland plants are limited by geography as well as soil type. Although the stemless thistle seems at times wilfully to haunt downland picnic sites to the exclusion of all other places, it is more severely confined by climate to the south of England. Bird's-eye primrose, on the other hand, is a plant of the northern hills, restricted to a belt of carboniferous limestone between the Pennines and the Scottish border. Being a southerner, born and bred, I had always longed to see this flower in the wild, the more so because I knew it to be one of the most exquisite of all our native species. Some time ago I was given a portrait of the bird's-eye, a watercolour original painted by the Countess of Aylesford in the 1780s. It is so ethereally pastel in its pink and grey shading, so daintily formed, that I used to assume it was a miniature – and a faded one at that – of something altogether more substantial in the field.

But that was about as solid an impression of the plant and its whereabouts as Tony and I had when we set out to search for them in Westmorland. I think we imagined they would be scattered unfussily about, like so many pink cowslips, wherever there was a patch of limestone grassland. We were, then, a little mystified when we failed to find any sign of them on the close-cropped turf of Orton Scar, a famous northern grassland site; and, trying another extreme, by their absence from the lush hay meadows nearby, which seemed to contain just about every other limestone plant in a warm quilt of purples and yellows. But then we had no real idea what *precisely* we were looking for. A dwarf in the short grass? A skulker in the tall? Something more sturdy and upstanding on the windswept heights? A check back in a book suggested that it had a special taste for damp, peaty soils that were flushed by calcareous springs; and the Ordnance Survey map showed there might be just such an area where a patch of moorland began abruptly about ten miles east of Shap Fell. We drove slowly towards it, and the higher we climbed the more the whole landscape bleached towards the colour of the limestone itself. The grass in the fields, the drystone walls, the dust in the wide drove-road, shone pale honey and silver under the hazy June sun. Migrating lapwing flew over, and calling curlews grazed in the newly cut meadows. The air, scented with hay and nectar, was so clear that we could see across 10 miles of burnished, silk-pelted hills. We felt that we were on the very top, the bare skull, of the fells.

The change, when it came, was quite perceptible: a darker, more bumpy field to our left; a flash of magenta from a clump of northern marsh orchids; the white bones of a sheep on the far verge. You learn not to ignore such portents when you are plant-hunting, and we stopped the car by the orchids. Less than 20 yards the other side of the wall we found our first bird's-eye primroses. It was an undeniably peaty place, full of rushes and red rattle. Yet the primroses seemed all to be growing on shorter turf, on ridges raised about an inch above the rest of the moor – perhaps where the soil was lighter and less waterlogged. They were much smaller than I had expected, but more delicately beautiful than I had dared to hope. They seemed, with their coral-pink flowers and dusty leaves, to have been formed out of the very stuff of the rock beneath. And they were to the life, in size and subtlety, the flowers in the Countess's painting.

Our expectations about wild flowers affect not only our perception of them but sometimes, I suspect, where they actually grow. Wild daffodils are, strictly speaking, a woodland plant in this country. Yet we think of them – and most often see them – as plants of open grassland. The great colonies at Farndale in the North Riding and Grasmere in the Lakes (Wordsworth's 'host') are national tourist attractions. We seem to prefer the cloth of gold to the scattered spangling amongst the trees. It is not hard to see how the wild daffodil should have metamorphosed into a grassland plant in these places. It is a species with a westerly distribution in

Bird's-eye primrose, in a high limestone
pasture near Shap Fell. June

Europe, and it will persist tolerably well on damp sites where the woodland has been cleared, or then again spread out from it into old, improved grassland. In more easterly regions, or anywhere where grassland is regularly drained or chemically treated, it is much more sensitive.

There is something of a mystery, then, about why there should be such an intense concentration in the area on the Gloucestershire/Herefordshire border centred around Dymock and Newent, which can hardly be said to have been free from the kinds of disturbance that normally obliterate daffodils. In the 1930s the area was so famous for its luxuriant, wild yellow fields that the Great Western Railway used to run weekend 'Daffodil Specials' there from London, and the flowers are still dense enough in places to transform the look of this 10 square miles of country in April. They are utterly promiscuous in their growth, crowding over waysides, across orchards, up the banks of underground reservoirs and the Ross Spur of the M50, and amongst the bracken in young conifer plantations. I have even seen a few plants clinging on in the churned-up mud of a pig-run. In places you can see the ghosts of old meadows or woods in the lines of daffodils tucked under the hedges of what is now ploughland. Seen at a distance these gold-rimmed fields can produce an odd optical illusion. Their yellow blaze is so sheer that the rings of flowers seem to be not so much circling the fields as suspended like chaplets from the nearer trees. It is the colour (or rather colouring) of the wild species that helps produce this effect. I first saw the Dymock colonies with Francesca Greenoak, an old friend and a perceptive observer of plants. She had never seen wild daffodils *en masse* before, and her notes of that first sharp impression caught perfectly their essential quality, which is a lightness and freshness quite absent from the more opulent garden varieties:

> The flowers themselves are lovely – taut, pert, two yellows; the yellow of the trumpet not turning green but arching right back to the papery bud-cover; the surrounding petals appear to be forward pointing in some (perhaps the early ones?) and stretched out in a pale star in others. In fields it looks as if they are

growing in bunches. Some back-to-back, looking outward – others alerted in one direction.

No wonder that people were once prepared to pay the train fare from London to admire and gather wild daffodils. We happened to learn, on this visit, the story of the other side of this annual transaction, from a vicar whose own churchyard was carpeted with the flowers. Apparently many of the local farmers used to regard the wild daffodils on their land as a valuable cash-crop. They would put up boards on their gates and charge visitors a bob or two to pick what they wanted. At the end of April the meadows went back to their normal business of growing hay. But that extra income must have preserved many from premature 'improvement', and no doubt led to daffodil bulbs being transplanted to holdings where they were not so common. This must have helped conserve the plant, and I have a feeling that a kind of 'daffodil consciousness' developed in the district, founded on the originally (but not exceptionally) dense colonies in local meadows and orchards, heightened by the influx of tourists, exploited unsentimentally at first by the pay-and-pick sales and probably a good deal of transplantation, and resulting, finally, in an evident local pride that the region had become the wild daffodil centre of England. The village of Dymock itself is a festival of daffodils in early spring, and bungalow gardens, churchyards and roadside verges alike are a mad jumble of narcissi, from the wild to the blowsiest of nurseryman's varieties. The parish, though it may not be to a Wordsworthian aesthete's taste, has most decidedly recognized and looked after its own.

There is one other curious tale of probable – though by no means certain – daffodil transplantation. In one of the few surviving ancient hay meadows in Suffolk, at Monewden, daffodils grow in a greensward that rivals the summer Dales' meadows for colour, with cowslip, snakeshead fritillary, green-winged and

OVERLEAF: *The blaze of wild daffodils in their heartland round Dymock, Gloucestershire. April*

early purple orchids, and, in early autumn, meadow saffron. But the daffodils are not, in this case, the wild variety, *Narcissus pseudonarcissus*, but the Van Sion cultivar, single-coloured, double-flowered, and first developed by a Flemish gardener in 1620. As far as is known, the Monewden meadows have never been ploughed or sprayed, and it is quite exceptional for garden plants to penetrate the tight cover of wild species that builds up over such long periods of stability. So how the Van Sion effected its entry had always been something of a mystery. But in 1973 a local botanist, P. J. O. Trist, tracked the plant back, along the paths and ditch-banks and hedge-sides where it also grows, to the local churchyard one mile away. There he found the daffodil growing conspicuously on three graves (dated between 1830 and 1857) all belonging to members of the Garnham family. The parish records show that this family owned the farm at Monewden for generations prior to 1899. That perhaps was its beginning, in a final tribute. But how the Van Sion made its mile-long journey from churchyard to Church Meadow (as it is called) is likely to remain as much a puzzle as the origins of the Buckinghamshire oxlips. It naturalizes well and may have found its own way along the footpaths and field-edges. But it was clearly a favourite of the Garnhams, a kind of family emblem, and perhaps they fancied seeing it not just as a tidy gravestone posy, but as a wilder workaday keepsake, in the setting of their favourite working meadow.

Not half a dozen miles from Monewden, there is another old meadow where fritillaries were the cash-crop. Just after the war, Mrs Queenie Fox used to allow visitors into her meadow at Framsden for a charge of a shilling. That was for the looking. You could pick one flower as a memento, and that was all. This says much for Mrs Fox's sense of responsibility (the meadow is now a Suffolk Trust reserve named in her honour), but also a good deal about the image of the fritillary itself. If the wild daffodil is seen as familiar, cheerful, gregarious, the snakeshead is exotic, alien, glamorous in a sinister sort of way, scarce, solitary, and, at times, seemingly invisible. Its most famous site is the meadow at the back of Magdalen College in

Oxford, where in most years it is in flower in time for the May Day ceremony on the college tower, when they 'do according to ancient custom, salute Flora every year on the first of May at four in the morning, with vocal music of several parts'. I have to say that I spent three years at Oxford and many spring mornings walking around Magdalen Meadow without ever once noticing a fritillary. I was less enraptured by flowers then, so perhaps there was some excuse. But, as I discovered later, the habit of overlooking fritillaries was nothing new, and said as much about the fortunes and 'presence' of the plant as about any personal blind spots.

When I went back to Magdalen years later for the express purpose of seeing the fritillaries, it still took me a while to bring them into focus. It was not that they were small or drab, though there was something reticent – sulky almost – about the way the mottled purple bells drooped down into the grass. It had, I think, more to do with their rather aimless scatter about the field, and an amorphousness that seemed a far cry from the sharp-cut brightness that we normally associate with the flowers of an English meadow. At a distance the fritillaries looked as if they had more in common with worm-casts than moon-daisies. It was only in close-up (we had permission to enter the meadow) that their rather sultry beauty began to take shape. The root name, *Fritillaria*, which De L'Obel coined in the sixteenth century from *fritillus*, a dice-box, is, oddly, the furthest from capturing the look of the plant. Gerard accounts for the name as deriving from 'the table or boord upon which men play at Chesse, which square checkers the floure doth very much resemble'. Yet the patches of purple, pale and dark, which adorn the petals are not in any sense as neat and separated as checkers. If you are close enough you will see they are not even purple, but a mottle of mulberry, lilac and the rusty brown of dried blood, with the patches of colour laid over each other, as if they were scales. One snakey feature, but by no means the only one. The unopened flower-buds are another, nipped into the shape of a snake's head. Lie beneath a cluster of flowers – this is the way to see them – and they will sway above you in the wind like a nest of cobras. If you have got this far, you will not miss the dagger-like petals pointed towards you, nor the venomously yellow stamens (forked, you will persuade yourself) slipping between them. Vita Sackville-West wrote of them as 'sullen and foreign looking, the snakey flower/scarfed in dull purple like Egyptian girls'.

Even in their local and vernacular names the flowers had reptilian, foreign, even diseased associations. In Shropshire they were dead men's bells; in the West Country, lepers' lilies, which was both a reference to the bells once carried by the afflicted and, perhaps, to an imagined resemblance between the livid blotches of the disease and the mottle of the petals. In the parish of Minety in Wiltshire they were toads' heads, and in parts of Buckinghamshire, frogcups. (There is a Frogcup Meadow marked on an 1803 map of Donnington in the Thames Valley.)

The fritillary has vanished from almost every one of these places in the last fifty years. Now restricted to some twenty-odd meadows, it could at the beginning of the century be found in twenty-seven different counties, from Kent and Hereford in the south to Staffordshire in the north. There were large colonies on the Duke of Wellington's Thames-side estate at Stratfield Saye in Berkshire and smaller ones in the Lea Valley, north of London. Yet, astonishingly, it was not recorded from the wild until 1736, when John Blackstone reported that a colony had been known for forty years in Maud Fields near Ruislip. Gerard's description was apparently based on garden specimens, for he wrote that, 'These rare and beautifull plants grow naturally wilde in the fields aboot Orleance and Lions in Fraunce, from whence they have been brought into the most parts of Europe.' The Magdalen flowers were not explicitly noted until 1785.

This seemed an odd oversight, and in his *Flora of Oxfordshire* (1886) Claridge Druce remarked that, 'It is not a little singular that the Fritillary, so conspicuously a plant of the Oxford meadows, should have so long remained unnoticed by the various botanists who had resided in or visited Oxford.' It seems so singular, in fact, that in recent years it has become something of a convention to regard the fritillary as a naturalized introduction, escaped or deliberately spread from the seventeenth-century gardens where it was so popular. There is no doubt that this did happen in many places (as it did with the wild daffodil) and maybe plants in

*Snakeshead fritillary. Magdalen
Meadow, Oxford, May Day*

Magdalen Meadow were one such instance, brought in from one of the more remote Oxfordshire meadows in the early 1780s. Who, after all, could resist the chance of setting such blooms so that they could be seen against the beige stonework of the great tower? Certainly if you compare Magdalen with some of the old meadows in Wiltshire it is easy to believe that the fritillaries there were given a helping hand. The grass around them is too coarse, other flowers too scarce. By contrast the spectacular displays in the more humdrum working countryside to the west are in meadows containing sometimes as many as a hundred different species. The finest of all, North Meadow at Cricklade in Wiltshire, is on Lammas land which has an unbroken history of hay-growing and common grazing going back 800 years.

This was not necessarily the kind of countryside that seventeenth-century botanists would have felt worth exploring. As for those residing in Oxford, suffice it to say that the university professor of botany at the time the Magdalen colony was 'discovered' was Humphrey Sibthorp, who reputedly only gave one lecture in forty years, and that not a very good one.*

I suspect that the reason why the fritillary was 'discovered' so late by botanists was not that it was deliberately introduced but that it had a very short, early flowering period and a restricted range, and even in the seventeenth century was already being reduced by agricultural change, particularly improved drainage. As has been all too obvious in the last fifty years, it is a highly sensitive plant. It prefers sites which are waterlogged during the winter, and, having corms which live for only about ten years, relies for its long-term survival on setting seeds, which can only be guaranteed in unploughed hay meadows.

A look at the fritillary's overall European distribution is very suggestive of a wild

---

* One current theory about the Magdalen population is that it was begun by introductions from the genuinely wild colonies in meadows at Ducklington, in the Windrush valley. The living of this parish was in the patronage of Magdalen College and the incumbent would have visited Oxford regularly.

origin. In Britain it has seemingly always been confined to the valleys of the Thames and its tributaries, and the river valleys of eastern England. On the continent it is centred around the Rhine Valley. Before the opening of the North Sea, these rivers were all part of a single system, and it is likely that the fritillary migrated north-west into Britain as these rivers formed in the wake of the melting glaciers. At this time, and for a long period subsequently, the fritillary must have found its natural home in very damp woodland clearings (a habitat in which it still grows in Europe). I have only once seen a fritillary under trees in Britain, a solitary plant escaped from the colony at Magdalen into a nearby thicket. It looked, I must say, much more at home than in the meadow, no longer a snake in the grass, but a woodland lily whose sultry bells had found their proper setting in the checkered shadows of the spinney floor.

PART FOUR

The Waste Lands

Most of Britain is covered by woods or fields and, given half a chance, the latter will revert rapidly to the former. But there is a third category of habitat where conditions are too extreme for either wild trees or cultivated crops, and which remains 'open' as a result of purely natural forces. These areas are amongst the most fascinating botanical hunting grounds of all, not least because amongst them are our last truly wild habitats, in the sense that they have been comparatively free from human interference. They are also often remnants (or replicas) of the great mosaic of open country that existed after the retreat of the glaciers. Because of this common ancestry (and what we might look on as certain shared character traits amongst their native plants), I have grouped them together under the heading of the waste lands, though there is not, at a first glance, much resemblance between them. They would have to include, for instance, mountain reaches too frequently under ice and snow to sustain the growth of trees, as well as all manner of sheer and rocky places at lower elevations: cliffs, gorges, ravines, limestone pavements. At another extreme would be the coast, where saltmarsh and dunes are regularly drenched by the sea and blown about by gales. There are permanently wet places inland, too – bogs, fens and swamps, natural lakes and rivers and their banks. Many surviving patches are very small, like some of the limestone crags above rivers in the Yorkshire Dales, or the damp 'slacks' that occur between old sand dunes.

The plants that have survived in these tiny oases of wildness – marooned, many of them, for thousands of years – have one overriding feature in common. They have all successsfully adapted to conditions of extreme stress, be it wind, fire, frost, flood, drought, or an almost complete absence of nutrients in the soil. They are, consequently, very tough but very specialized. Out of their own fields they can be quite at a loss, like finely tuned athletes. They can be astonishingly persistent in their traditional sites but never seen away from them. In this respect they are fundamentally different from another group of tough plants we have already looked at (the 'weeds'), which are characteristically unspecialized and ephemeral. It is the dogged survival of the long-distance runners in the waste lands that can make discovering – especially *re*-discovering – them such an exciting business.

Some twenty species of flowering plant became extinct between the beginning of the seventeenth century (when the first reliable records were made) and the 1970s. One of these was the handsome fen ragwort, *Senecio paludosus*, whose tall stems of saw-toothed cottony leaves and flat-topped yellow flower clusters once graced many fens in East Anglia. It was first recorded by John Ray in 1660, and at the end of the eighteenth century still occurred widely in Norfolk, Suffolk, Cambridgeshire and Lincolnshire, and perhaps also in Cheshire. Its decline seems to have begun in the first half of the nineteenth century, probably as a result of the extensive drainage works which were then under way in the fens. The last record substantiated by a specimen is from Wicken Fen, Cambridgeshire, in August 1863, though notes from later writers suggest that it may well have hung on, here and there, into the early years of this century. Then, in July 1972, a small clump was discovered in a ditch inside its ancestral territory in Cambridgeshire. The botanist who found it was able to keep his excitement sufficiently in check to observe that the flowering stems carried '8–25 capitula'.

There are a number of possible explanations for fen ragwort's re-materialization. It may have recolonized the area with seed blown in from the continent. (It is still comparatively widespread in Holland.) It may have been deliberately introduced, though it is hardly likely this would have happened with such an esoteric plant without the planter putting his or her action on record. A more credible explanation is that the species was not extinct at all, though this still begs the question of the circumstances under which it survived. Had it persisted in small numbers as a fully flowering plant because, as with so many other species, its remote colonies had been overlooked, or because at a casual glance it could be mistaken for another abundant fen-ditch species, the perennial sow-thistle? Perhaps, but this cannot have been the case at the particular site where the plant was found in 1972. This was a new ditch, dug as recently as 1968. The most likely answer is that the plant had sprung from seed lying dormant in an undisturbed

OVERLEAF: *Heather moorland. A man-made waste resulting from forest clearance on impoverished soil. Strathclyde, August*

143 ·

layer of the peat in which the ragwort anciently grew. When the new ditch was excavated it may have brought the seed to light, so to speak, and at the same time created an artificial habitat sufficiently like a 'natural' fen to ensure the survival of the flowers after germination. This has happened with other scarce local species, including the fen violet, *Viola stagnina*, which has been known to reappear suddenly after scrub clearance (and associated ground disturbance) in nearby Woodwalton Fen.

Many commoner wetland plants seem to be able to appear quite quickly in newly wet sites. The edges of abandoned gravel pits, canals, even flooded mine subsidences, can be rapidly colonized by species such as marsh marigold, yellow flag, hairy willowherb, yellow loosestrife and common reed. Many of these species (water plants being adapted, naturally enough, to the peculiarly mobile qualities of water) have seeds which are floatable, or which can be carried on the feet of water birds. But the more exacting plants of ancient wetland wastes depend for the most part on their habitats remaining intact, and even the reappearance of fen ragwort could not have occurred if the damp sedge-peat in which it grew, and which sheltered its dormant seeds, had been destroyed.

Persistent wetness is one kind of extreme. Drought is another. The lowest rainfall in Britain is over central East Anglia, where there is sometimes as little as 17 inches a year. The heart of this stretch of country is a large area of chalky, glacial sands known as the Breckland. The soil, such as it is, is quick to heat up and quick to cool, and the little rainfall it receives drains away rapidly. Together, climate and geology have combined to produce the closest approximation to desert conditions to be found in these islands. There may have been areas on the light, impoverished soils of the Brecks that were never completely wooded, and certainly the forest cover that did exist was cleared early and easily by neolithic settlers, leaving a wilderness of sand 400 square miles in extent. It was shifting sand, too, prey to the unchecked winds that hurtled about the treeless wastes. In 1668 a south-westerly gale blew up a sandstorm that buried the village of Santon, and blocked the Little Ouse for half a mile.

Most of the Breckland is now submerged under a more sombre cloak of conifer plantations and military bases, its wildness tidied and tamed by pine wind-breaks and rows of asparagus. But if the feel of the old desert has largely vanished, some of the plants that grew in it still survive in field corners and on waysides, and can remind you of the time when travellers in the Breckland used to start their journeys well before dawn to escape the full heat of the sun whilst their coaches were being dragged through the deep sand. Some of the species that grow together in the Brecks are not found again in any quantity until you reach the arid steppe-lands of central Europe. Three exquisite annual speedwells – the Breckland, fingered and spring – are amongst these and can be seen occasionally in bare stony places and at the edge of arable fields. They bloom early in the spring before the thin soil has begun to dry out.

In the few places where there are still inland sand dunes, you may find a handful of species more often associated with the coast. Sand sedge grows here in the orderly straight lines formed by its horizontally extending root system. Sand catchfly, which grows on the beaches of Suffolk, 50 miles to the east, also crops up. I have seen its tiny pink flowers and swollen sepal tubes in great numbers on a deeply rutted roadside verge just yards from the edge of the A11 by Lakenheath Airbase, showing again how stubbornly the rare species of these wastelands will cling to their aboriginal territories even if it means taking advantage of quite artificial replicas of their natural habitats. Another catchfly unique to the Breckland, *Silene otites*, tends to grow where there is a short grass cover, as do two other local specialities, maiden pink and grape hyacinth.

But perhaps the most fascinating of the Breckland species is the spiked speedwell, *Veronica spicata*, whose spires of intense blue flowers are now restricted to just four localities. It was once much more widespread, and in 1915 W. G. Rainbird Clarke wrote of a site 'where there are over 1,400 plants in a very limited space'. The Breckland spiked speedwell is a short creeping variety, referred to by taxonomists as ssp. *spicata*. A larger and more upstanding sub-species, ssp. *hybrida*, occurs more frequently in limestone outcrops in Wales. It is tempting to think that the geographical isolation of the two colonies – the one growing on calcium-rich rocks in an area of high rainfall, and the other on the thin, dry sands of East Anglia – actually caused the evolution of the two types until you learn that they grow side by side on the continent. It is quite likely that they grew similarly intermingled in post-glacial Britain, and were only pushed to ghettos at the limits of their respective tolerances by the extension of the forest cover and, later, by the taking in of so much wasteland for cultivation. One of the sites for the western spiked speedwell is the strange, steep hump of limestone in Montgomeryshire known as Craig Breidden. Here it grows with sticky catchfly, rock stonecrop and rock cinquefoil, a plant whose good looks (it is something like an herbaceous alpine strawberry) has resulted in its moving in rather disconcerting quantities off the hill and into local gardens. All these species are rare enough individually in Britain, but as a community they do not occur again for nearly 600 miles, on rocky wood-edges in central Germany. Another species which grows in this area of Europe is the pink, *Dianthus gratianopolitanus*. In Britain it is a very exclusive plant, confined to limestone cliffs in Somerset. It was first noticed on the 'Chidderoks' in 1724, and has been known as the Cheddar pink ever since. It has probably been more heavily collected by gardeners than any other native plant, and is now completely protected by law. The colonies that do survive are almost all on inaccessible rocks, and the Cheddar pink is one of the few flowers which, for its safety as well as your own, is best looked for through binoculars.

Coastal cliffs also have their specialities, though it is probably the commoner species that we associate more with these sites. The massed drifts of thrift, sea campion, spring squill, bluebell and primrose on the granite cliffs of south-west Britain in May are one of the most glorious sights our flora has to offer. Their habit of growing in snug, rounded clumps is part of what makes them so attractive, yet it is a strictly functional feature, designed to protect the plants from wind damage and dehydration on these exposed sites. It is odd, given their obvious resilience,

Yellow loosestrife. A rapid colonizer of new wetlands in regions where it is already established. Norfolk Broads, August

that these species so rarely crop up in any quantities on granite slopes inland. No doubt the ubiquitous sheep has something to do with this. But flowers growing on coastal cliffs may actually benefit from the minerals blown their way in salt spray, and which are in short supply (except on limestone) inland.

But it is never easy to tell whether the characteristic plants of the shoreline are concentrated there because they have a particular need for salt, or because they have evolved special defences against it. Either way salt – persistent, corrosive, dehydrating salt – is a major factor in shaping their life-styles. Almost every feature of their habitats conspires to threaten the freshwater supplies of seashore species. The plants are exposed to fierce, drying winds. They grow in substrates – rock, shingle, sand – which have virtually no water-retaining powers. They are repeatedly soaked with saline spray or actually submerged in seawater, which, to inland plants, would be as terminal as pickling.

Some species defend themselves with thick coverings on the outside of their leaves. Sea holly's is waxy, sea sandwort's like glossy latex. Marram grass, one of the first colonizers of sand dunes, rolls its leaves up into a tube to minimize evaporation during wind and drought. The leaves of many shoreline plants – most notably glasswort, sea purslane and shrubby seablite – are succulent, which conserves water in the event of drought, and helps dilute the salt which they take in willy-nilly.

Meanwhile, their roots will be probing the rock or shingle for underground – and usually less saline – water reserves. The roots of yellow horned poppy and rock samphire regularly go down more than 6 feet. Some species, such as shrubby seablite, have in effect the capacity to root *upward*, sending out new shoots from their growing tips when these are submerged by gale-blown sand or shingle. Perhaps the most remarkable adaptation of all is in the maritime variety of the curled dock, whose withered stems form a kind of protective tent over its new shoots during the winter.

What is probably the best-known of all seaside flowers, the thrift or sea pink, has a whole battery of defences: deep tap-roots, fine grass-like leaves, and a dense tufting habit to hold in damp air. It would be too fanciful, I think, to imagine that these frugal, water-saving devices had anything to do with the plant's name. This has been current since at least the sixteenth century, and was well enough known for the plant to have figured as a pun on the back of the old threepenny bit.

THE LAST RESORTS

Thrift is one of the most widespread of all seaside plants, growing on shingle, sand, the higher reaches of saltmarshes, and even on the walls of cliff-top cottages. It is also one of a small group of maritime plants that are equally at home on mountains. (It is curious that there are not more such plants, given that the two habitats were physically linked rocky sites in late glacial times and share many similarly extreme conditions.) I have never seen thrift on a mountain, but, knowing it on grey rock against a dark Atlantic sea, I can imagine what it must look like growing in the clear light above the clouds, and can understand why mountain flowers are the supreme attraction for so many botanists. It is not just the perfectly compact form and sharp colours of alpines that make them so magnetic. It is hard not to be tempted by those remote fastnesses, and not to feel a touch of envy for those early botanists who made their hazardous way up to them, and saw, for the first time on these islands, those bright tufts in the crevices. There is, too, the seductive possibility that you might do the same yourself and, on some high ledge, stumble on a flower that had hidden unnoticed for 12,000 years. At the very least there is the chance of seeing anew, in some wilder setting, flowers you know from the comfort of your own rockery, as Professor J. H. Balfour did on his expedition to Ben Lawers in 1847:

> There is, moreover, something peculiarly attractive in the collecting of alpine plants. Their comparative rarity, the localities in which they grow, and

OVERLEAF: *Saltmarsh and sea lavender. North Norfolk, July*

frequently their beautiful hues, conspire in shedding around them a halo of interest far exceeding that connected with lowland productions. The alpine *Veronica* displaying its lovely blue corolla on the verge of dissolving snows; the Forget-me-not of the mountain summit, whose tints far excel those of its namesake of the brooks; the *Woodsia* with its tufted fronds adorning the clefts of the rocks; the snowy Gentian concealing its eye of blue in the ledges of the steep crags; the alpine *Astragalus* enlivening the turf with its purple clusters; the *Lychnis* choosing the stony and dry knoll for the evolution of its pink petals; the *Sonchus* raising its stately stalk and azure heads in spots which try the enthusiasm of the adventurous collector; the pale-flowered *Oxytropis* confining itself to a single British cliff; the Azalea forming a carpet of the richest crimson; the Saxifrages with their white, yellow, and pink blossoms clothing the sides of the streams; the *Saussurea* and *Erigeron* crowning the rocks with their purple and pink capitula; the pendent Cinquefoil blending its yellow flowers with the white of the alpine Cerastiums and the bright blue of the stony *Veronica*; the stemless *Silene* giving a pink and velvety covering to the decomposing granite. . . .

And so it goes on, the scenes merging in your mind into one fabulously ornamented alpine garden, in which, once you have reached it, you have but to stroll about from one brilliantly encrusted rock to another. . . . The less said about Tony's and my feeble attempt to find such a castellation in the air the better, though the story has a moral of sorts. We badly misjudged both the scarcity and inaccessibility of the British mountain flora, and our own patience and climbing abilities. We started (responsibly, we thought) on some modest slopes in the Pennines, found some pleasant mountain pansies at about 1000 feet and nothing at all higher up. We tested ourselves on Helvellyn in late June, but were driven back at about 2000 feet by a temperature in the mid-eighties with only the memory of the brilliant green fuzz of parsley fern on the scree for our pains.

Then I read about Beinn na h-Uamha, a mountain in western Argyllshire where an extrusion of calcareous basalt (a variety of solidified volcanic lava) brought scarce alpines down to about 1500 feet. This sounded altogether more within our reach, and we started out on what we imagined would be a leisurely amble one afternoon in early July. It turned out to be our most fearful climb. Beinn na h-Uamha is a little-used hill with few paths, and we had to scramble and slither up through sodden waist-high heather, with our feet continually sliding away on hidden granite slabs or down into boggy holes in the peat. As we groped our way up what seemed endless, exhausting miles of moorland, with not an alpine in sight, we began to wonder if we were on the right mountain. We realized with mounting desperation that, even if we were, we had not the slightest idea what basalt looked like.

We finally reached it, in stepped cliffs at the top of the mountain. The great fissured sheets, like slabs of spongy, rusted metal ('fossilized cow-pats' retorted Tony), were obviously what we were meant to look at, but we were in no state to appreciate their finer features. Our legs were trembling from the climb, and flakes of basalt were beginning to break away under our feet. And, adding final insult to what we felt sure was imminent injury, none of the choice alpines we could now see very clearly, growing in beaded rows along the crest of the ledges, was actually in flower. Purple saxifrage, moss campion, alpine meadow-rue were over; rose-root and all the other saxifrages (including what I think was *Saxifraga nivalis*) still to come. Only alpine lady's mantle – common in these parts – was in full bloom.

I cannot deny that we were glad to begin our journey down. But, though we had not been able to share Professor Balfour's glittering vision, standing (or rather quaking) on that crumbling cliff in the company of those vegetable hermits was the most impressive physical lesson we could have had on the essential character of our mountain flora. This flora has been reduced to a fragmentary collection of plants capable of living in conditions of extreme privation in inaccessible pockets of mineral-rich rock; the precise combination of gradient, moisture and soil stability in these sites favouring just one or two species above all others. Most of our alpine species once grew here in greater quantities (and of course still do at higher altitudes on the continent) but they were progressively blanketed out by forest, robbed of soil salts by our high rainfall, grazed away by sheep once the woodland had been converted to pasture, and finally hounded by collectors.

Thrift or sea pink. Pembrokeshire, May

Alpine lady's mantle. Highlands, July

The next day, feeling depressed and tired, and rather wanting to *enjoy* some flowers, we decided to potter about in search not so much of mountain-plants as plants on mountains. We chose the range of hills that tumble gently down into Loch Linnhe, partly because they looked accessible and easy to walk, and partly because, by a sea loch in the Gulf Stream, they might support a few mountain species at low altitudes. Indeed we did find some of the commoner species, especially yellow saxifrage and roseroot, in great abundance near sea level. It was a day of the purest Highland light, no wind, the sky a shining opalescent blue. Tony set up his camera about 50 feet above the loch and we lounged there most of the day, gazing out across the clear, still water. Far out in the Loch red-throated divers crooned and gannets dived for fish. The day wore on. I held a white parasol over the camera to shield the gelatine filters from the spray of a waterfall near our chosen saxifrage. A seal, barking quietly, swam up the loch, and, one hour later, swam back again.

Later, as we ate our lunch amongst a homely Scottish mixture of harebell and wild thyme, we decided – I hope not purely from a guilty sense of our failure on the high tops – that for mountain botanizing to be more than a random treasure hunt you needed to be both a geologist and an athlete. We had no pretensions to being either. I think we both felt, on that perfect day, that our preferences were with flowers that had more intimate human associations than the lonely alpines, or at least a more ordinarily comprehensible setting.

How pleasant then, to find a place as agreeable as our lochside where it was possible to enjoy mountain flowers as something more than bejewelled prizes at the end of an endurance test. There are a few such places in the British Isles, and the most famous of all is the Burren in County Clare. This is the ultimate limestone landscape, not far short of 200 square miles of shattered rock, scoured bare for the most part by glaciers and eroded by the high rainfall into a maze of limestone slabs, pavements and sugar-loaf terraces that look like nothing so much as a scaled-down version of the Arizona desert. You would think it was barren as well as bleak, yet it is one of the richest farming areas in Ireland, and in winter farmers bring their cattle on to the Burren to fatten them on the young hazel shoots and fine grasses. The browse may be thinly scattered, but it does flourish in every month of the year in the humid Atlantic climate, and the cattle do well on it. Perhaps they benefit from the high mineral content in the grass, or from the great variety of other plants they must chew up as well. For this is the other paradox of the Burren – the bizarre cohabitation of species that are more familiar in different settings and very different company. You see mountain avens on a beach, spring gentian in a wood, heather growing on seemingly bare limestone. You begin to wonder how such species could ever have been brought together, as if they had always been confined to the highly specialized habitats in which we now know them. But you do not need to spend long in the Burren to be persuaded that such mosaics, though now the exception, were once the rule, and that the real question is not how these species came together here, but what factors prevented their being driven apart. Seen in this light, as an improbable relic of late-glacial Britain, the Burren plant mix becomes more comprehensible. The Burren, botanically speaking, is the best of most possible worlds. It is mild throughout the year, frost-free in winter, and rarely afflicted by drought. The high rainfall drains quickly away through the porous limestone, giving little chance for peat to form in the cracks in the limestone. Trees, as we have seen, will grow here, but there is too little humus and too much wind to allow them to reach any substantial size. The Burren is a landscape of moderation, with so little in the way of extreme conditions that little in the way of plant life has been driven away. The only species that are conspicuously scarce are those needing continuously waterlogged conditions and the rank, weedy species that are associated with high nitrate content in the soil.

You should start your exploration of the Burren in late May, from the seaward side. The slabs of limestone, capped with turf here and there, are covered with a bewildering mixture of plants – bloody cranesbill, thrift, early purple orchids, and with them tufts of spring sandwort, mountain avens (*Dryas octopetala*), with its

May in the Burren

Burnet rose, the most exquisitely scented of all our wild roses. The Burren, May

twists of silky seed-plumes developing at the same time as the flowers, and the deep sapphire shine of spring gentians. And you may be lucky enough to see the one plant with a truly Irish botanical name, the pure white variety of the spotted orchid known as subspecies *O'kellyii*.

As you climb inland the paths are lined with more *Dryas*, with tufts of hoary rock-rose, and with little colonies of what to me is the most pleasing plant of the region, the mountain everlasting, with its woolly leaf rosettes and tiny daisy flowers, white in the male and suffused with pink in the female.

Then the ground flattens, and the Burren heartland begins – a landscape of Celtic cromlechs, derelict farms, hazel groves, and great limestone pavements broken up by deep cracks (known as grikes). It is these grikes that provide the excitement here. Each one has its own unique collection of plants. One will be thick with species more usually found in fens – hemp agrimony, water avens, meadow-rue. Another has glossy hart's-tongue ferns and dark red helleborines. A third has a giant ash tree – only it is growing horizontally, winding its way along the course of the grike. Many of the grikes carry gnarled trees growing in this fashion – blackthorn, buckthorn, yew, spindle – impossible to date, but which may have been creeping amongst the rocks for centuries, leaning away from the wind, grazed back every time they try to grow vertically. I spoke earlier of the hazel groves that come up no higher than your chest; yet here there are primeval woods that never reach above ground level, whole communities ranging from the mosses and ferns in the lowest, damp depths, through flowering herb roberts, bluebells and strawberries, to this naturally bonsaid forest cover at the top – all growing in a trench at your feet.

By this time you will have lost your botanical bearings, until you find one of those magical places in the Burren where all these tableaux come together. This will quite likely be at one of the turloughs – mysterious lakes which rise and fall according to the level of the water table in the limestone. I have seen one such place – and I am sure there are many more – that I would wish anyone the joy of finding. I could not say exactly where it is, but then I would not want to, for its enchantment lay in its unexpectedness, as well as in its curious familiarity, its *rightness*. The pool was surrounded by bushes of shrubby cinquefoil, already covered with their yellow cistus-like flowers. Behind them were slabs of warm rock, draped with burnet rose. Beyond these every patch of ground was different. There was a damp hollow, perhaps a less frequently flooded turlough, with fen violet, adder's-tongue fern, water germander, and a copper-leaved eau-de-cologne-scented variety of water mint. There was a stretch of turf with a collection of plants that could have come straight from our native Chilterns – salad burnet, thyme, harebell (in bud), and five sprightly fly orchids. There was alder buckthorn in one grike, juniper in another, and an ash topiaried by the cattle to the shape of a perfect hemisphere.

We lay on the ledge nearest the pool, and watched the burnet rose flowers opening in the sun. As their pure soft scent blew over us in the breeze, over the shining pool and white rock, we understood why this foreign place was so familiar. It was, in its balance of wildness and order, colour and form, the perfect garden of our imaginations.

FLOWERS, PRESENT AND FUTURE

In the spring of 1977, a Suffolk botanist exploring some of the old narrow lanes in the parish of Shelley noticed that one of them was bordered with quantities of wood anemone. This was a pleasantly unexpected find, as the anemone is very scarce outside woodlands in East Anglia, and it led another local, Edgar Milne-Redhead (of black poplar fame), to look more closely at the site. He found that the hedge behind the verge consisted almost entirely of overgrown coppice stools of an even scarcer species, the small-leaved lime (which was a common tree in south-eastern Britain in prehistoric times). It is unusual to find two such sensitive woodland species growing together in the open, and suggested that the hedge might once have been part of an ancient wood. After more investigation, in records and in the field (which incidentally led to the discovery of a wild service tree in the hedge), the mother-wood was traced on an eighteenth-century map. Its northern edge, about 600 yards long, coincided exactly with that part of the lane bounded by the lime hedge. The remainder of its 40 acres must have been grubbed out early in the nineteenth century, as there is no sign of it on the first edition Ordnance Survey map made in 1838.

Such hedges – and there are probably many more examples than we realize – have become rather evocatively known as 'woodland ghosts'. It seems to me a very apt term, suggesting as it does not just the previous existence of something more substantial, but a lively contemporary presence, a cheating of time. . . .

In this sense a good deal of our countryside consists of botanical ghosts, the roadside verge echoing the vanished pasture, the ditch surviving as a shadow of the fen. And there is something else that the metaphor should remind us of. There is, it is becoming increasingly clear, no ecological equivalent of resurrection. When ancient woods or meadows are destroyed they have gone for ever, and if we wish to have any reminders of them at all we must hang on to their remains, however ghostly, at all costs. Whatever we may do in the way of restoration and replanting, new habitats can never be *replacements* for the ones we are losing, either in terms of the flowers that grow in them or the cultural associations, built up over thousands of years, whose richness I have tried to suggest in this book.

That is not to say that we should not welcome additions to our plant-scape. One of the most vital things about the natural world is, precisely, that it is *not* static. Although most of the changes we see in it today (even benign ones) are inevitably ephemeral, some new arrivals are already beginning to leave their mark in our mythology of plants. 1976, for instance, will be remembered as the year when a single plant of the Mediterranean mirror orchid, *Ophrys bertolinii*, was found in flower in a patch of old downland in Dorset. The nearest native locality for this species is 600 miles away in southern France, and opinions are divided between those who like to imagine the tiny seeds wafting in high thermals across the Channel during the idyllic summer of 1975, and those who suspect a local orchid farmer, well known for scattering seeds about the countryside.

White water-lily in the Lake District.
Little Langdale, June

There are no such doubts about the origins of many colonies of another southern European species, the fairy foxglove. This brilliant pink alpine has many fans, but none more devoted than the married couple who carry a stock of its seeds with them on their travels round Britain, planting them out on any suitable limestone site.

Echoes of the old magical respect for plants have found modern expression, too. Many farmers still spare holly trees – potent plants both in pagan and Christian traditions – when they grub out their hedges, even, it seems, in preference to oak. (Though I should like to know whether a similar regard was paid to the fig tree that not so long ago burst out of a tomb in a Watford cemetery. I know what a medieval herbalist would have made of it.)

It is so much more satisfying when plants make their own decisions about where to grow. Perhaps I am morbid, but I find it very appropriate that the most uncompromisingly baleful growth of deadly nightshade in our parish is to be seen at one of our traditional accident black-spots – the place where the neolithic ridgeway joins the Roman valley road, the epicentre of a host of local legends about ghostly coaches, night riders and headless donkeys, and where, most recently, a dual carriageway was dug into the chalk and provided the opportunity for the nightshade's seeds to come to life.

When a new habitat like this is firmly colonized by a new species, we have an authentic extension of the ancient pattern of association. Oxford ragwort is now as familiar an inhabitant of industrial landscapes as the bluebell is of old woods. It was introduced to this country in the mid-eighteenth century, when Linnaeus planted it out in the Botanic Gardens in Oxford. It seemed to have escaped one summer in the 1790s. Its seeds took root in nearby college walls, and gradually edged their way to Oxford station and to the wide swathe of open ground cut out by the Great Western Railway. It seemed to find the stony foundations of the permanent way very much like its native European habitat on volcanic scree and, using the expanding railway system as a beach-head, rapidly colonized the whole of industrial Britain. The story of its spread has even begun to accumulate its own folklore. Claridge Druce described a rail journey he took with some of its downy seeds, which wafted into his carriage at Oxford, one Victorian summer afternoon, and disembarked at Tilehurst, 20 miles down the line.

Walls are perhaps the most seemly and stable of all man-made habitats, and have been colonized by a wide range of species. One survey recorded 286 species on the walls of south-east Essex alone. (Their more subtle preferences were not noted, but a study made of the plants growing on church walls in central France found the most luxuriant growth on Protestant churches which, being less diligently attended than the Catholic, were damper and more conducive to vegetable growth.)

But the most botanically exciting of all man-made habitats are abandoned quarries, particularly those on chalk or limestone. This has its ironies, given the devastation they often cause to a landscape, but it is perhaps not such a surprising development if we consider superficial similarities between a worked-out quarry and the open post-glacial landscape. Very few old quarries are ever allowed to fulfil their potential, of course. The vast majority are exhausted of their parent rock, insensitively landscaped, and filled with rubbish, or are simply too remote from other wild habitats for any colonization to take place. But the few that, by some chance, were prematurely abandoned early this century and then just left alone cannot fail to remind you, either as landscapes or as plant communities, of some of the inland limestone gorges in Somerset and the Dales.

Noar, Hill Common in Hampshire scarcely resembles our vast modern earth-works, but it was a quarry of a kind, where the commoners of Selborne once had the right to dig for stone and chalk. They made gentle diggings, perhaps because the surrounding chalk grassland was simultaneously being used for sheep grazing. As a result, there were always corners of undisturbed turf from which the bare chalk could be recolonized. The quarry was abandoned in the middle of the last century and now carries a marvellously rich community of plants, including nine species of orchid, and a good deal of juniper scrub – the first shrubby colonizer of the bare chalk just as it was 10,000 years ago. And there is also in late

Oxford ragwort in Oxford, just a few hundred yards from the Botanic Gardens from which it began its colonization of Britain's urban wastelands in 1974

Harebell. Scotland, July

summer a fine show of harebell, the great survivor. This is almost certainly the Campanula whose pollen has been found amongst the first late-glacial plant remains. It will grow on almost any dry, open, relatively undisturbed site, from mountain tops to dune grassland at sea level. It is as happy on acid heather moors as on chalk downland. I have seen it thriving on the top of an ant-hill in a flooded water meadow, and growing so closely packed on a railway embankment that from a fast train the flowers looked like a flash of painted china.

The harebell is, to me, perhaps the most perfect of all British wild plants. Its paper-thin sky-blue flowers make gentians look vulgar, and are as beautiful in the form of a single, swaying bell in a sea of bracken as in a host on a cliff-top. Their great tolerance – but a tolerance with limits – is a vivid symbol of the deep relationship with plants that we have maintained for thousands of years but could now so easily lose.

Guide

In this short section I have gathered together notes on references, further reading, access to sites, fieldwork etc., so it is, in effect, a guide to further, *practical* investigation by the reader.

A few basic background texts:

For local names, folklore etc., see Geoffrey Grigson's scholarly and discursive *The Englishman's Flora* (1958, new edition 1987). A recommended list of 'standard' English names (which has been largely followed in this text) is published by Butterworths as *The English Names of Wild Flowers* (1974).

For distribution maps see: Alastair Fitter, *An Atlas of the Wild Flowers of Britain and Northern Europe* (Collins, 1978); *Atlas of the British Flora*, Botanical Society of the British Isles (BSBI) (Nelson, 1962, 2nd ed. 1976). Also any local or county flora, of any date, that you can lay your hands on. Many nineteenth-century floras crop up in antiquarian booksellers' lists and give fascinating accounts of the early history and past distribution of our plant life.

(The BSBI, co-publishers of the *Atlas* above, is *not* a society exclusively for professional botanists. It organizes many meetings and outings, publishes a very readable newsletter and should be supported by anyone interested in our wild flowers. The address of the honorary general secretary is: White Cottage, Slinfold, Horsham, West Sussex RH13 7RG.)

INTRODUCTION

The Conservation of Wild Creatures and Wild Plants Acts, passed in 1975 and 1981, prohibit the uprooting of any wild flower without the permission of the owner of the land on which it is growing. They also give complete protection – prohibiting picking as well as uprooting – to a number of exceptionally rare British plants, including the military orchid, Cheddar pink, ghost orchid, lady's-slipper orchid and spiked speedwell (all mentioned in this book). For the early history of the military orchid see *Wild Orchids of Britain*, V. S. Summerhayes (Collins, 2nd ed. 1968). This is one of the excellent New Naturalist series, which includes some of the best introductions to plant ecology in print. Try also to find a copy of Jocelyn Brooke's maverick *The Military Orchid* (Bodley Head, 1948), an autobiographical volume loosely based on a lifetime's search for the plant. If you wish to see the plant for yourself, the Suffolk Trust for Nature Conservation has an open day each June at its reserve at the military orchid's other British site – an abandoned chalkpit in a Forestry Commission plantation! The Suffolk Trust has a commendably outward-looking policy towards its reserves, and also holds open days at the oxlip coppice (Bulls wood) at Cockfield and the ancient meadows at Monewden and Framsden mentioned in the text. Details of the open days and membership from the Trust's registered office at Park Cottage, Saxmundham, Suffolk P17 1DQ.

John Gerard's vast *The Herball or Generall Historie of Plantes* (1597) was the first widely read book on the plants, wild and cultivated, to be found in Great Britain, and is referred to often in the text. Although much of it is a rather shameless (and by no means accurate) plagiarism of a translation of Dodoen's *Herbal* (1578), Gerard communicates his own delight in plants so effectively that the book is still a joy to read. In 1633, the London apothecary Thomas Johnson published a 'revised and enlarged' edition, discreetly correcting most of Gerard's mistakes. This edition is available in a contemporary facsimile (Dover, 1976).

HISTORY

The best simple introduction to the history of the British flora is Winifred Pennington's *The History of British Vegetation* (English Universities Press, 1969).

Then, in rough order of difficulty: *Britain's Green Mantle*, A. G. Tansley (Allen & Unwin, 2nd ed. 1968); *The British Islands and their Vegetation*, A. G. Tansley (Cambridge, 1939) – an ecological survey as well as a history; *History of the British Flora*, H. E. Godwin (Cambridge, 2nd ed. 1975). See also: Phil Colebourn and Bob Gibbons, *Britain's Natural Heritage: Reading our Countryside's Past* (Blandford, 1987).

WOODS

Oliver Rackham's books are essential reading for an understanding of the way that human use and natural growth interact to shape the structure and plant life of woods. *Hayley Wood: Its History and Ecology* (Cambridgeshire and Isle of Ely Naturalists' Trust, 1975) is a detailed study of a single old coppice in Cambridgeshire. *Trees and Woodland in the British Landscape* (Dent, 1976) is a more general study, and includes an excellent chapter on fieldwork in woods (interpreting boundaries, names, earthworks, indicator plants, etc.). More recent and comprehensive works are: *Ancient Woodland: its history uses and vegetation in England* (Dent, 1980) and *The History of the Countryside* (Dent, 1986). The most accessible and useful aid to fieldwork is a set of first edition Ordnance Survey maps – first published in the early years of the nineteenth century – which are now available in facsimile from David & Charles.

Good areas to go looking for ancient woods, and their very particular plants, are: the wealds of Kent and Sussex; the chalk hangers of Hampshire; north Dorset; the border country between Chepstow and Shrewsbury; the Chilterns; south Suffolk and north Essex; the belt of the east Midlands from Northampton to Louth in Lincolnshire; and the Lake District. But remember that the mention of any wood (or any other site) in this book is no guarantee of public access. Wayland Wood, for example, is a private reserve of the Norfolk Naturalists' Trust. (Enquiries concerning permits and membership to 72 Cathedral Close, Norwich NR1 4DF.)

HERBS

There is a multitude of books, old and new, about the medicinal uses of plants, but fewer about the herbals themselves. Three good surveys of the literature are: Eleanour Sinclair Rohde, *The Old English Herbals* (1922; Minerva Press edition, 1972); Agnes Arber, *Herbals: their origin and evolution* (Cambridge,1939); and, for a remarkable glimpse of the illustrations in early manuscript herbals, Wilfrid Blunt and Sandra Raphael, *The Illustrated Herbal* (Frances Lincoln, 1979).

Christina Hole, *British Folk Customs* (Hutchinson, 1976) contains notes on surviving plant-based rituals, including tree-dressing, mistletoe-hanging and beating the bounds. Sites and dates of ceremonials are included.

BOUNDARY TREES

Read Gerald Wilkinson's two elegantly written books, *Epitaph for the Elm* (Hutchinson, 1978) and *Trees in the Wild* (Stephen Hope, 1973). Also, J. H. Wilkes, *Trees of the British Isles in History and Legend* (Muller, 1972) and all Oliver Rackham's publications. R. H. Richen's *Elm* (Cambridge, 1983), gives a fascinating account of the history of local elm varieties.

Some 6-inches-to-the-mile Ordnance Survey maps mark important boundary trees.

HEDGES

When dating hedges remember that the formula (number of tree species per 30-yard stretch equals age of hedge in centuries) only applies to tree and shrub species. You must not count climbers like bramble and honeysuckle, nor any tree growing outside the structure of the hedge. Try and sample a number of randomly selected stretches for a more accurate result. For a thorough account of the technique and an excellent survey of the history and ecology of hedges, see Pollard, Hooper and Moore, *Hedges* (Collins, 1974). Those readers who are interested in the more esoteric reaches of dating should also seek out *Hedges and Local History*, published for the Standing Conference for Local History in 1971, which includes, amongst other fascinating essays, David Elliston Allen's paper on the rough ageing of West Country turf-banks from an analysis of the bramble micro-species growing on them.

WEEDS

Unquestionably the best guide to the British weed flora is Sir Edward Salisbury's classic *Weeds and Aliens* (Collins, 1961), out of print, somewhat out of date, but still unsurpassed. For news of the latest additions to the immigrant flora (and their bizarre modes of entry, from packets of lentils to cushion stuffings) read the botanically uncompromising but always entertaining 'Adventive news' in the BSBI's newsletter.

GRASSLANDS

There are rather few books on the botany of old grasslands, but see Eric Duffey *et al., Grassland Ecology and Wildlife Management* (Chapman & Hall, 1974).

There are, incidentally, species confined to old grasslands much as there are those limited to ancient woods. For instance, species such as pignut, pepper saxifrage, fritillary, meadow saffron, great burnet, meadow thistle, green-winged orchid, saw-wort, devil's-bit scabious, dropwort and globe flower, though they can be found individually in other habitats, only occur *as a group* in unimproved meadowland which has long been managed for hay.

WASTELANDS

Three more Collins New Naturalist volumes will be your best guides here: J. E. Lousley, *Wild Flowers of Chalk and Limestone* (revised ed. 1969); Ian Hepburn, *Flowers of the Coast* (1952); John Raven and Max Walters, *Mountain Flowers* (1956).

Most of the Burren is open country, and there is customary (and sometimes legal) access to most of Britain's high mountain tops. (It is worth while, incidentally, investing in a cheap altimeter, as you are unlikely to find any true alpines below 2000 feet.)

Index

Also from Chatto & Windus

OPERATION OTTER
Philip Wayre

Otters are wild, fascinating, and endangered. But thanks to Philip Wayre and his wife Jeanne they are at last returning to England's waterways. From his first sighting of an otter in a Norfolk dawn, this wonderful story follows Philip Wayre's dream – from his early filming of otters to the setting up of an otter reserve and, finally, the culmination – the successful and safe release of groups of young otter cubs into the wild.

Operation Otter is moving, appealing and practical, full of irresistible photos and a wealth of information about the otter itself.

The Secret Life of The
NEW FOREST
Eric Ashby
Introduction by Richard Mabey

In this enchanting book of colour photographs, the secrets of one of Britain's oldest and most beautiful forests are revealed. The wild and natural aspects of the Forest through the changing seasons – from giant oaks to deer and ponies, from fox cubs, badgers and pigs to woodpeckers, rare orchids and butterflies – are observed with infinite patience, love and more than a touch of genius by a man who has photographed wildlife for over fifty years and lives deep in the New Forest.

SOMETHING IN A CARDBOARD BOX
Tales from a Wildlife Hospital
Les Stocker

Les Stocker is the James Herriot of the wildlife world. In their back garden in Aylesbury, he and his wife Sue run a wildlife hospital where, day and night, pathetic furry bundles arrive in cardboard boxes.

This is the irresistible account, packed with illustrations, of ten years of wildlife rescue, full of heartbreaks and hilarity – and a mine of invaluable information.

THE COMPLETE HEDGEHOG
Les Stocker
Foreword by John Craven

Everyone loves hedgehogs. Here is the most comprehensive book ever written about this endearing mammal, one of nature's greatest assets.

Les Stocker presents, in this fully illustrated, magical book, information about the hedgehog's history, mythology, distribution, habits and habitat, as well as practical advice on how to unroll a hedgehog, how to encourage one to your garden, what to do about orphan hedgehogs and how to treat casualties.